Schurman Rock
A History & Guide

JEFF SMOOT

FOREWORD BY JIM WHITTAKER

FOURTH HILL
PUBLISHING

Schurman Rock: A History & Guide

Fourth Hill Publishing
1725 SW Roxbury Street, Suite 2
Seattle, WA 98106-2752
fourthhillpublishing@gmail.com

ISBN-13: 978-0692068014
ISBN-10: 0692068015

Clark Schurman's article, "Monitor Rock," (*The Mountaineer*, Volume Thirty-One, Number 1, December 15, 1938) is reprinted with permission of The Mountaineers.

Front and upper back cover photos of Mountaineers' climbing practice, 1947, by Bob and Ira Spring, courtesy of The Mountaineers. Lower back cover photo of WPA laborers starting to work on Monitor Rock, 1938, from Camp Long collection.

All uncredited photos by the author.

CONTENTS

No one has been seriously injured or killed while climbing on Schurman Rock that we know of. Please don't be the first! Climb safely, at your own risk.

CLIMB AT YOUR OWN RISK!

THIS IS, IN PART, A GUIDE TO ROCK CLIMBING, so I must warn you that climbing, even on Schurman Rock, is dangerous and has inherent risks that cannot be avoided no matter how careful you are. Climbing is a dangerous sport where you may be injured or even killed. As the signs posted at the rock say: Climb at Your Own Risk.

Although there have been very few if any serious accidents at Schurman Rock, there is still a risk. The biggest risk is probably a child falling, being knocked over the edge by another child, slipping on loose gravel while playing carelessly on top of the rock, or being hit by a falling climber or climbing gear. Children and dogs should be kept away from the rock when others are climbing. Adult supervision of children is highly recommended!

As a general rule, don't climb higher than you are willing to fall, learn how to fall in a way that minimizes your chances of injury, and use a bouldering pad, spotter, toprope, and/or helmet when appropriate for the sake of safety. This is not a climbing instruction book. Nor is this book a substitute for sound judgment learned through experience. Please learn climbing techniques, safety, and rope-handling methods from a qualified instructor or guide. Camp Long offers climbing as part of its outdoor programs and for groups; check their upcoming programs or ask about booking a group session on the rock.

No warranties, either express or implied, are given that the information in this book is reliable or accurate. There are no implied warranties of merchantability as to this book. The author and publisher assume no liability for accidents that happen to, or injuries suffered by, users of this book. Use of this book indicates the user's assumption of risk that it may contain errors or fail to warn of known or foreseeable dangers, as well as the acknowledgement that climbing is dangerous and that the user is solely accountable for his or her own abilities to climb in a safe and responsible manner.

Clark Schurman on the summit of Mount Adams, 1938.
Photo: Camp Long collection.

Monitor Rock is humble. I hope there is no effrontery in what has been done . . .

–Clark Schurman, 1938

Rappelling during a Mountaineers outing at Monitor Rock, 1947.
Photo by Bob and Ira Spring, courtesy of The Mountaineers.

FOREWORD

SEVERAL YEARS AGO, I was invited to speak at a celebration of the 75th Anniversary of Schurman Rock. I was pleased to do so. Schurman Rock, which I know as Monitor Rock, is where I first learned to climb. The "rock" was just a 25-foot-high mountain of rock and concrete at a park near my home in West Seattle. It was close by, and became a great place to scramble and learn how to use holds and climbing techniques. My brother, Louie, and I first climbed on the rock in 1941. We learned the basics of climbing there, how to belay, rappel, and climb chimneys and vertical walls, and soon applied these techniques to a climb of The Tooth, a 5,605-foot-high peak near Snoqualmie Pass, our first real mountain. It scared the hell out of us, but we were reassured by the training we had received at Monitor Rock. We lived to tell the tale, and before long we climbed a lot more mountains including Mount Rainier. We were both hooked on climbing, and made climbing the focus of our lives. Many years later, I was fortunate to be invited on an expedition to Mount Everest, and on May 1, 1963, I became the first American to reach the summit of Everest. I have always been mindful, though, of where my climbing career began. If not for my early climbing experiences on Monitor Rock, I might not have gone on to climb Mount Everest.

Because of this, I was pleased to learn that someone had written a book about Monitor Rock. The author, Jeff Smoot, sent me an advance copy of *Schurman Rock: A History & Guide*, which I thoroughly enjoyed, particularly the history of the rock and stories about the people who climb it. It is a great introduction to climbing on Schurman Rock, and a good introduction to climbing in general, a book worth reading by anyone who wants to climb anything, anywhere. All the basics are covered for beginning climbers to learn how to climb on the rock, knowledge that is best gained through a good read instead of trial and error with severe consequences. And reading the book brought back some wonderful memories, including this one:

One day in the summer of 1943 at the rock, Tom Campbell, a Mountaineer and World War II veteran, and a wonderful guy, was instructing Louie and me on the basics of rock climbing. Tom had had a hand blown off in the war and it had been replaced with a gloved artificial duplicate that screwed into a device implanted in his forearm. Being a true mountaineer, he had a hook made that could also be screwed onto his arm. The hook enabled him to use the tiniest features of the rock for good handholds. He could climb places that no one else could. Tom was on top of the rock and Louie and I were climbing just below the "summit," when there was an earth-shattering scream that scared the hell out of us. We both almost peeled off the wall. Then someone shouted, "Oh my God! It's a hand! It's somebody's hand!" When Tom had unscrewed his hand and screwed in the hook, he had just left the hand on a ledge at the base of the wall. When asked later why he had done that, he said, "Because it was handy."

There are indoor climbing walls now, and a lot of climbers are climbing indoors. I think that's great, because climbing is such a great sport. But if you know me, you know my motto: "Go play outside!" We're so lucky to be able to get out into nature and do something amazing on this magical planet. I tell people to get out onto the edge and out of their comfort zone; it's where you learn the most. Because you're pushing yourself and learning your boundaries, learning what you can do and what you can't. If you're not living on the edge, you're taking up too much space.

So, if you're reading this book, get out of the climbing gym some sunny afternoon and head over to Schurman Rock. Even though it's just a little pile of rocks cemented together, it holds a unique place in the history of climbing. And, as I can assure you, climbing Schurman Rock can lead to high adventure.

Jim Whittaker
October 2017

INTRODUCTION

THE HISTORY OF URBAN CLIMBING IN SEATTLE IS UNIQUE. Artificial wall climbing was born here. Although climbers have been climbing on buildings and other structures since at least the late 1800s, Seattle was the first city in the world to have a man-made climbing wall built purposely for climbing as sport: Monitor Rock, constructed by the Works Progress Administration in 1938-39. The rock was renamed Schurman Rock in 1957, in honor of its designer, Clark Schurman, following his death in 1955. In 1976, a more-modern climbing wall was built on the University of Washington campus. And in 1987, the first known commercial climbing gym in America, the Vertical Club, opened in Seattle, spawning a worldwide industry. Schurman Rock and the U.W. Rock are still standing; Vertical Club is now Vertical World, one of several climbing gyms in the Seattle area.

Over the years, climbing gyms have drawn climbers, young and old, to the "great indoors" and away from the outdoor walls. Schurman Rock doesn't seem to attract a lot attention compared to the climbing gyms or the new Mountaineers Wall at Magnuson Park, but it is still one of the most-often climbed artificial walls in the city. Nearly every day, dozens of kids of all ages scramble to the top of the rock to take in the view; the more adventuresome among them try it by a more-challenging route, then another, and another; some have to be dragged away under protest. This would no doubt have greatly pleased Clark Schurman.

Schurman, a Scoutmaster, climbing guide, and wilderness leader, designed Monitor Rock with kids in mind, to provide a controlled environment to safely teach climbing skills to Boy Scouts and other youth groups. As he described it in his article, "Monitor Rock," published in *The Mountaineer* journal in 1938, his climbing rock was intended as "a boulder to teach as many rock-climbing skills as might be built into one mass within a given budget, and yet, that would be as safe for an unsupervised group of wandering small boys as their own dooryards." Schurman bragged that, even as of 1938, before the rock was officially completed, "scores of untutored lads have swarmed over [the rock] without a sign of trouble," dashing up the easy way and then "proceed[ing] to greater difficulties by the hour." This still happens at Schurman Rock on an almost daily basis.

Bouldering on Schurman Rock.

On a recent spring day, I arrived at the rock in the morning to find it already swarmed by a pack of unsupervised 9- to 12-year-olds—a dozen kids in sneakers, clambering over nearly every face, buttress, and chimney. These boys and girls, part of a school group camped overnight at Camp Long, were not your typical pack of "wandering boys"—who might be as inclined to climb the rock as to throw rocks at each other. This group was enthusiastic, adventuresome, and quite serious about climbing the rock. Not satisfied with climbing up the "staircase," they were soon scampering up the pinnacle, chimneys, cracks, and buttresses, one after the other. A couple of the girls, discouraged that their tennis shoes seemed to slip off the rocks too easily, took off their shoes and climbed barefoot up some of the steepest walls. This, too, would no doubt have greatly pleased Clark Schurman, although he might have scolded them for climbing without a rope and adult supervision—or chased them out of the park as he was known to do when neighborhood children snuck into Camp Long to play.

This book originated as a chapter in my book, *Pumping Concrete: A Guide to Seattle-Area Climbing Walls* (1996). That obscure book is being republished with a more-complete history of climbing walls as a cultural phenomenon. As that project progressed, it seemed that, given its relative historical importance as the first climbing wall ever, Schurman Rock might deserve its own small book, not only about the rock but also about the people who have climbed and continue to climb it, and about its creator, as a history of the rock and surrounding park, its cultural significance, and also as a user's guide to climbing on the rock, so future visitors can better appreciate the historical and cultural significance of Schurman Rock and also experience it as it was meant to be experienced—by climbing it.

Primarily, this book is intended to provide a brief history of Schurman Rock and Camp Long, and a biography of Clark Schurman—not an exhaustive history or biography, but sufficient to give the reader a fairly thorough background on the Seattle climbing community prior to construction of Monitor Rock, Schurman's vision of the rock, its design and construction, and its use over the ensuing decades. It also includes a chapter of stories about the people who climb on the rock: two brothers who had to be dragged off the rock by their grandfather, a group of kids who discovered Schurman Rock during a visit to Camp Long one summer, an expert boulderer who stopped by during a recent visit to Seattle to see what the rock is all about, a retiree dusting off his old climbing shoes and heading to the rock one evening to see if he still "has it," and many more.

Of course, one cannot publish a book about Schurman Rock or any other climbing wall—real or artificial—without including the best part: climbing. To that end, a few dozen climbing routes on the rock, including several of Clark Schurman's original "short bits" and some more-modern bouldering test pieces, are included.

One might scoff at the notion of publishing a guidebook to climbing on a relatively obscure artificial climbing wall. Fair enough. Given that Schurman Rock is an artificial rock, designed to teach climbing to kids and not for development of contrived boulder problems or other ego-gratifying pursuits, a guidebook to climbing on Schurman Rock may seem silly and, in any case, something not to be taken too seriously. After all, the rock was designed for teaching, safety, and for "mountain appreciation as opposed to personal exhibitionism" as Schurman put it, and that's what it is still used for. At least, nobody is climbing on Schurman Rock to show off, get their name in a climbing magazine, or be featured in a *National Geographic* special. It's just a small man-made boulder climbed mostly by unsupervised kids, the author chiefly among them.

Still, in his "Monitor Rock" article, Schurman published a guide of sorts to twenty-two distinct routes and training exercises on the rock, so others could come and try those "short bits" and better experience and appreciate what the rock had to offer. This book, which includes several of Schurman's old "routes" and many later boulder problems, follows in that tradition. The "routes" included here are not so much to show off what has been done, but to reveal what is possible if you use your imagination, and to inspire climbers of all ages to appreciate and enjoy the serious fun that can be had climbing on Schurman Rock.

I first climbed on Schurman Rock in the mid-1970s and am still at it forty years later, spending a few hours bouldering there once or twice a week when the weather allows. My early visits were as a teenage boy first learning to climb; later, I came with friends to hang out and get in some bouldering in between hacky sack sessions; then it was serious bouldering, working out the hardest problems possible as training for "real" climbing. Now that I am older and not quite as ambitious as I once was, I come more for a quick workout and a place to escape to for an hour or two away from home or the office. I could join a climbing gym, but in the time it would take me to drive to the nearest gym and back, on Schurman Rock I can get in the equivalent in vertical footage of an ascent of Half Dome. Besides, I'm one of those old-school climbers who started climbing before there were climbing gyms; my preference remains to climb outdoors if possible, sunlight or storm, in the company of birds, bees, and the occasional stray climber who might happen along, even if it's only on a little pile of rocks cemented together.

Thousands of people have climbed on Schurman Rock over the years, and there are thousands of stories. This book is not intended to be a comprehensive history, nor a mere catalog of boulder problems, but a blend of both that is informative, entertaining, and useful, I hope, for those who are interested in this small slice of local climbing history.

Certainly, the history of Schurman Rock and the story of Clark Schurman's life are interesting and important, but given that the rock was designed and built for climbing, the focal point of this book should be and, therefore is, climbing. I am sure Clark Schurman would have agreed.

Clark Schurman surveys the site prior to construction of Monitor Rock,
1938. The boulder he is standing on was left in place and incorporated
into the rock. Photo: Camp Long collection.

1.

A BRIEF HISTORY OF SCHURMAN ROCK

SCHURMAN ROCK IS REPUTED TO BE THE FIRST man-made climbing structure in America. It may well be the first artificial climbing wall in the world built with the sport of climbing in mind. A 1970 British Mountaineering Council publication, *Artificial Climbing Walls*, the first-known book on the subject, acknowledges that Schurman Rock was the first purpose-built artificial climbing wall, ahead of the adjustable wooden walls built in France in the 1950s and the school and university walls built in England in the 1960s. Of course, climbers were already climbing on artificial walls in the late 1800s, but those walls were sides of buildings, such as the famed "Barn Door Traverse" on the side of a stone barn at Wastdale Head in the Lake District, not walls built purposely for climbing training and practice, which did not appear in England until 1960. Prior to that, there were many gymnastic training apparatus that incorporated rope or ladder climbing and even a documented early artificial climbing wall circa 1820 that was used for military training exercises. However, Schurman Rock, designed by Clark Schurman and built by the Works Progress Administration between 1938 and 1939, is credited as the first artificial climbing wall anywhere in the world intended specifically for mountaineering instruction and practice.

Yet, in his 1938 article in *The Mountaineer*, Schurman belies the myth: prior to Monitor Rock, there was a "wooden 'cliff' at Troop 65's Camp Stanley," a "useful mountaineering gym" consisting of scaffolding on trees that had been used since 1929 to teach safe climbing techniques to Scouts and other invited guests.

Either way, in the words of Lou Whittaker, who first climbed on Monitor Rock with his brother, Jim, in 1941, "Clark Schurman was ahead of his time."

Whether or not it was the first artificial climbing wall ever, Schurman Rock is still a historic structure, certainly the first of its kind in America. That it was conceived, approved, and built during Depression-era Seattle is something of a miracle of the right people being in the right place at the right time to take advantage of a once-in-a-lifetime opportunity. The climbing rock probably would not have been built in Seattle during the Great Depression—or perhaps at all—but for the fortuitous timing of New Deal programs which included formation of the Works Progress Administration (WPA), and establishment of a youth camp in Seattle that came to be known as Camp Long.

A view of Clark Schurman's clay model for the climbing rock at Camp Long, 1937. Photo: Camp Long collection.

The New Deal was a series of Depression-era federal programs enacted during the presidency of Franklin D. Roosevelt between

1933-38. It included public works projects such as the construction of Grand Coulee Dam in Eastern Washington. These programs focused on relieving unemployment and poverty, recovery of the economy, and reformation of the financial system to prevent a repeat of the economic conditions that led to the Great Depression, the worst economic downturn in the history of the industrialized world. The Depression began with the stock market crash of 1929 and officially lasted until 1939, although the U.S. economy did not fully recover until after World War II.

Another view of Schurman's clay model for the climbing rock.
Photo: Camp Long collection.

The New Deal was controversial, and created a political split between the "liberals" who supported its humanistic and labor-friendly programs, and "conservatives" who opposed it as an "enemy of business and growth." Despite opposition, most of Roosevelt's New Deal policies were implemented. The "First New Deal" (1933-34) dealt primarily with financial reforms to shore up the banking crisis and provided funds for relief operations in states and cities. The "Second New Deal" (1935-38) implemented a variety of labor and relief programs, including the Wagner Act, Social Security Act, U.S. Housing Authority, and Fair Labor Standards Act, as well as the WPA and Civilian Conservation Corps (CCC).

The WPA, later renamed the Works Projects Administration, was formed in 1935. It employed millions of workers during the Great Depression to carry out public works projects across the U.S., making the federal government the largest single employer in the country. The WPA and other Second New Deal programs were highly controversial, however, and they were fervently opposed by conservatives. Following the economic downturn of 1937-38, Republicans and conservative Democrats joined forces to oppose them, and by the early 1940s they succeeded in shutting down some of the New Deal programs including the WPA and CCC. Fortunately, Camp Long and its new climbing rock were completed before these programs were eliminated.

———

Located on a 68-acre parcel of land originally slated for use as part of a golf course, Camp Long was conceived and developed by Ben Evans of the Seattle Park Department, Seattle Park Board member Archie Phelps, Superior Court Judge William G. Long, and Clark Schurman, with the assistance of several local juvenile character-building agencies, to create a place for organized youth groups to learn outdoor skills.

The history of Camp Long begins with a phone call from Phelps to Long in 1937. In addition to his position on the Park Board, Phelps was acting as a liaison representative of the city in the construction of the West Seattle Golf Course. Recognizing a unique opportunity, Phelps called Judge Long and, as Long recalled it years later, said, "There is a sixty-eight acre corner of the golf course tract that is not being used for golf. I have stopped the cutting down of trees because I think it would make a wonderful campsite for the Boy Scouts of West Seattle. I wish you would come over and take a look at it and see what you think."

Long, a longtime juvenile court judge and youth advocate, was typical of early twentieth-century reformers who sought to solve the "boy problem," to save adolescent urban boys from the corrupting influences of urbanization and industrialization and guide them along the proper path which, they believed, could be best accomplished by introducing boys to the challenges of wilderness. Cities had rapidly grown in the early 20th Century as people moved from rural to urban areas in search of jobs. But, as cities grew, so did crime and poverty. Concern over the plight of dislocated urban youth became a national conversation. Long, an avid outdoorsman who enjoyed fishing and hiking, had spent most of his career fighting juvenile delinquency. The idea of creating a wilderness camp in the city instantly appealed to him as a possible alternative to incarceration of wayward youth.

The Parade Ground in 1938 (top) and 1939 (bottom).
Photos: Camp Long collection.

Soon, Long and Phelps were tromping around on the golf course tract, surveying the acreage, fighting their way through brush, nettles, briars, fallen trees, and across a swampy bog. It was perfect. Long, who referred to the tract as a "jungle," thought it had great potential, not just as a camp for the Scouts of West Seattle, but for youth throughout the city.

Long and Phelps brought in a group of Boy and Girl Scout and Camp Fire Girl leaders, who were all soon bushwhacking through the briars, brush, and swamps. They were also impressed with the possibility of turning the tract into a youth camp, as was Evans, another ally on the Park Board. A committee of seventeen representatives from each of the youth groups in Seattle was quickly formed for the purpose of planning the urban wilderness camp project.

WPA workers starting to work on Monitor Rock, 1938.
Photo: Camp Long collection.

Schurman, already a well-known Scout leader who had developed a wilderness camp in North Seattle for Scout Troop 65, and who was also an expert in camping and mountaineering, was selected to draw the plans for the project and serve as its first director. Schurman and Evans conducted a nationwide search for similar projects developed in other communities, from which Schurman prepared an initial plan for the camp that was unanimously approved by the committee.

While Schurman made up plans for the park, which included a climbing wall, Long and Phelps took action to ensure that the plan became a reality. Long had tenaciously lobbied for and, using his influence as a Superior Court judge, won approval of use of the unused golf course tract as a youth camp. Then, further leveraging their connections and influence, Long and Phelps set about executing Schurman's plan.

With the nation still mired in the Great Depression and the economic downturn of 1937-38 just underway, it seemed that funding for the camp's infrastructure and construction would be difficult to come by. So, the pair engaged in "persuading, maneuvering, finagling, scrounging, snaffling," and what Long referred to as "benevolent larceny," to raise funds and gather building materials for construction of cabins, a lodge, and Schurman's climbing wall. Through Phelps's "bull-dog persistence," the Park Department was persuaded to put up some money, and the WPA was induced to furnish manpower to match the city's funding.

With the tract and modest funding secured, the project was set in motion. Construction of the camp began in 1937. The Lodge, the camp's main building, was built using stones intended for the repaving of East Madison Street. The rectangular granite blocks were originally used as ballast in the holds of ships that sailed into Seattle to pick up goods; the ballast blocks were offloaded as the ships were filled with goods bound for other ports, and used to pave many of Seattle's streets. Some of these stones eventually "found their way" into the Lodge and other Camp Long infrastructure including the Glacier. Wood from an old school building ended up in the lodge and cabins, and lumber from an abandoned CCC camp was also "quietly transported" to Camp Long. While this was going on, Phelps was elected to the King County Board of Commissioners and had a sawmill built for the county; before you knew it, more lumber had "made its way" to the camp. Originally, only three cabins were planned; tents were to be used elsewhere. However, after the first three cabins were completed in 1938, it was discovered that there would be more than enough material available to build more cabins, and seven additional cabins were constructed with more rustic design features including overhanging roofs and capped stone fireplaces.

Monitor Rock under construction, 1938. Note The chimney and overhang on the right, which were walled in c. 1941. Photo: Camp Long collection.

As if all of this was not enough, a nursery just happened to be in receivership in Superior Court that had a lot of ornamental trees in stock of doubtful value on the market. Somehow, Judge Long was able to persuade creditors of the nursery to donate the trees to the project, which provided most of Camp Long's initial foliage.

Some looked askance at the shady methods used by Long and Phelps to build the camp, but others viewed it more pragmatically. Sheila Brown, Camp Long's current Director, put it this way: "My understanding is that they were crusty guys who believed they were doing a really good thing for young people. It was the Depression years; nobody had any money. If stuff wasn't used by somebody else and you could make use of it, you were just being smart."

Although Long and Phelps had to use creative means to acquire materials to build park infrastructure, some federal funds were provided, in addition to the labor furnished by the WPA. Most of Camp Long's infrastructure, including Schurman Rock, was built with WPA labor. No doubt, the participation of the U.S. government in the construction of the camp was aided by Eleanor Roosevelt, who became involved during a visit with her daughter who lived in Seattle at the time. According to Evans, Mrs. Roosevelt "took a liking to the area and to the idea of preserving it... and she gave us wonderful support all the way through." The First Lady was reported to have attended the opening ceremony for Camp Long in November 1941, although other sources suggest she visited the camp prior to its completion and was not in attendance at the formal dedication.

Monitor Rock near completion, 1939. Photo: Camp Long collection.

Even though funding and infrastructure were in place to create the camp, there was opposition from the community. Some objected to the park's use as a wilderness camp, contending that the tract should be used as a more traditional community park that everyone could use, with facilities for more typical community activities— football, baseball, and tennis. Here, Schurman rose to the occasion, maintaining a strong stand against all activities except wilderness activities—camping and climbing, period.

Another battle was fought over access to the camp. Some in the community felt the camp should be open to any and all who wished to use the space, and not only for Scouting and other supervised youth group activities. Again, Schurman advocated strongly that the camp be closed and participation in camp activities must be under the guidance and direction of a responsible adult leader.

Without Schurman's advocacy, Camp Long might be just another city park; instead, it became and remains today a wilderness oasis hidden in a corner of the urban sprawl of one of the country's fastest-growing cities.

A Mountaineers group practicing on Monitor Rock, 1939.
Photo by Othello Phil Dickert, courtesy of The Mountaineers.

Part of Schurman's vision for the new wilderness camp—perhaps the keystone of the whole project as far as Schurman was concerned—was to build an artificial "mountain" that incorporated every potential climbing problem into its design, to have a place to provide climbing instruction for Scouts and other youth groups. He first sketched out a design, then built a clay model. Once his design was approved and the project was started, Schurman assisted (or got in the way of, as he put it) WPA workers during construction of his "dream rock" and accompanying "glacier," a larger feature located adjacent to the climbing rock designed for snow and glacier climbing instruction and rope-management practice. The rock was originally named Monitor Rock, because climbing instructors could monitor their students from all sides of the structure and "warn, remind, advise, and instruct" them as they climbed.

Monitor Rock was completed in 1939; the Glacier in 1940. With its two artificial climbing walls, Camp Long for several decades was home to the most cutting-edge climbing training facility in the world. Camp Long was officially dedicated on November 8, 1941, and named for Judge Long. Of Camp Long, then Seattle Mayor Earl Milliken said, "This magnificent recreation project exceeds any of its kind in any city of the United States." Indeed it did. Even today, Camp Long remains a unique urban wilderness area dedicated to outdoor and environmental education, instruction, stewardship, and leadership, providing many underserved and at-risk youth with their first outdoor experiences.

In 1957, Monitor Rock was renamed Schurman Rock as a memorial to Schurman following his death in 1955. Schurman served as Chief Climbing Guide guide on Mount Rainier from 1938 to 1941 and as a well-known, even beloved, Scout leader for more than twenty years. Schurman loved mountaineering for all that it had to offer, and his rock stands as a legacy to his vision. Since its completion in 1939, Schurman Rock has been climbed by thousands of climbers young and old, and has been used by generations of Scouts, beginning climbers, youth groups, mountaineering clubs, and search-and-rescue groups, not to mention countless children of all ages who seem to flock to the rock on any given sunny day, scramble to the top, and take in the view.

Prior to Schurman Rock, Seattle climbers had "Big Rock" (sometimes called "Glacier Boulder," later called "Wedgwood Rock"), a 19-foot-high erratic boulder located north of the University District, to use for climbing practice. Boy Scouts had use of their climbing structure at Camp Stanley, and could sometimes also be seen clambering up or dangling from various abutments, retaining walls, and overpasses in the city. However, for the most part, the Mountaineers and Boy Scouts chiefly used Wedgwood Rock for climbing instruction courses up until 1941, before the surrounding farmland was sold to a real estate developer and the boulder was closed to climbing. Wolf Bauer, who immigrated with his family from Germany to Seattle in 1925 at age 13 and later took up climbing as a Boy Scout, learned to climb here and taught climbing to Explorer Scouts on Wedgwood Rock. Through Scouting, Bauer received a membership in the Mountaineers. (Back then, you had to be recommended for membership or specially invited to join.) In 1935, the same year he made the first ascent of the Ptarmigan Ridge route on Mount Rainier, Bauer started the Mountaineers' first climbing course, which utilized Wedgwood Rock in its training in addition to nearby peaks in the Cascades. Within a year, Clark Schurman had joined the Mountaineers and become heavily involved in its climbing instruction programs.

A Mountaineers group practicing on Wedgwood Rock, 1941.
Photo: Lloyd Anderson, courtesy of The Mountaineers.

The timing of the completion of Monitor Rock could not have been more fortuitous. With Wedgwood Rock no longer available for climbing by the early 1940s, Monitor Rock became the only climbing wall in the Seattle area aside from overpasses and other infrastructure, and remained so until 1976, when the University of Washington completed its outdoor climbing wall and Spire Rock was constructed in Spanaway. Although not intended to replace

Wedgwood Rock, and not particularly designed for adult climbing groups, Schurman's rock allowed a seamless transition for climbing training after Wedgwood Rock was closed to climbing. Despite a report that it was bulldozed under during housing development, Wedgwood Rock is still there, a neighborhood icon that remains closed to climbing. According to the Seattle Municipal Code, climbing on Wedgwood Rock is subject to a $100 fine.

Although the loss of Wedgwood Rock was bemoaned by Seattle climbers, Monitor Rock was, in fact, superior to the real boulder in several respects. By definition a polylith—a megalithic structure composed of many small boulders cemented together—Monitor Rock stood approximately 20 feet tall and 100 feet around, slightly larger than Wedgwood Rock. Monitor Rock was designed to resemble a rock peak or large boulder, with a main summit and two detached towers. Schurman designed the rock to provide a place to practice every climbing technique then known, and it included slabs, steep faces, overhangs, chimneys, and a couple of boot-width cracks for climbing, as well as places to practice rappelling, running belays, rope work, and rescue techniques. Its companion feature, the Glacier, was designed to teach and practice other facets of mountain travel, including scrambling, snow travel, and glacier climbing techniques.

As originally configured, one could learn and practice a variety of climbing techniques and situations on Monitor Rock, including face climbing, layback, chimney, finger traverse, foot traverse, *à cheval*, tabling (manteling), belaying techniques, rappelling, Prusik, lasso, and the ever-popular shoulder stand. At the time it was designed and constructed, jamming in cracks (aside from basic boot-crack and chimney techniques) was all but unheard of, and as a consequence Schurman Rock has no real cracks to speak of where one could practice finger-, hand-, or fist-jamming, although layback, hand stack, knee bar, and Gaston techniques are possible.

The rock's climbing "routes" consist almost exclusively of face climbing on mostly smaller "cling holds" (what face holds were called back in Schurman's day) and larger "gift-holds" as Schurman called the various big blocks and ledges, as well as the many "wrinkles," "discolorations," and other minor features of the rock.

Fred Beckey climbing on Monitor Rock, 1939.
Photo: Lloyd Anderson, courtesy of The Mountaineers.

Schurman proudly introduced Monitor Rock to the climbing world in his 1938 article published in the *Mountaineer* journal, and the Mountaineers and other invited groups began using Monitor Rock *en masse* soon after it was completed—even before Camp Long was officially opened. Mountaineers groups that included Wolf Bauer, Ome Daiber, Lloyd and Mary Anderson, and Fred and Helmy Beckey were among the earliest users of the rock. Lloyd Anderson, who with his wife Mary founded Recreational Equipment Inc. (REI), soon conscripted each of the Beckey brothers on first ascents of important peaks in the North Cascades, and in 1942 the Beckeys— Fred a mere nineteen years of age, Helmy just seventeen—made the second ascent of Mount Waddington in British Columbia's Coast Range, a major mountaineering feat that shocked the climbing world.

Although the Beckeys were already capable climbers before the rock was built, one imagines that their training sessions on Monitor Rock allowed them to perfect the rock climbing skills that permitted them to climb Mount Waddington with apparent ease.

A Mountaineers group on Monitor Rock, 1941.
Photo: Lloyd Anderson, courtesy of The Mountaineers.

Of course, Monitor Rock was ostensibly built for and primarily used by Scouts and other youth groups, often under Schurman's strict-but-enthusiastic leadership. Among the Scouts who climbed on the rock early on were twelve-year-old twin brothers, Lou and Jim Whittaker, who learned to climb on Monitor Rock in 1941. "It was … hardly Mount Everest," according to Jim, "but a great place to scramble and learn holds and climbing techniques." The Whittaker twins learned techniques at Monitor Rock that they soon used on their first real climb, The Tooth, a 5,604-foot-high rock peak near Snoqualmie Pass. "We 'leapfrogged' up the route," Lou recalled later, "as we had been taught at Monitor Rock."

Schurman located his rock atop a hill with an unobstructed view of Mount Rainier, eighty miles to the south, with the hope of inspiring those who learned to climb there to climb "the Mountain."

The Whittaker boys were certainly inspired; they climbed Mount Rainier together in 1944, and later became climbing guides at Mount Rainier. Jim went on to become President of REI, the first American to summit Mount Everest in 1963, and leader of the first successful American expedition to K2; Lou founded Rainier Mountaineering Inc., for many years the sole guiding concessionaire at Mount Rainier, and led the first successful American ascent of the North Col route on Everest. If your first climbing experience was on Schurman Rock, you are in good company.

In years following its construction, Schurman Rock was used primarily by youth groups, climbing programs, and mountain rescue organizations to teach basic climbing and rescue skills. Until 1984, Camp Long was still open only to organized youth groups but closed to general public use. This did not dissuade many local climbers and neighborhood kids from "sneaking in" and climbing on the rock, even though Clark Schurman used to chase off any neighborhood kids he found in the park.

Although Camp Long was officially closed to the general public, neighborhood kids flocked there after school to scramble on the rock and play rock tag. Bob and Jean Wagner, Bill Long, Jr. (Judge Long's son), and Boyd Bentrot served as directors of Camp Long after Clark Schurman, from the late 1940s to the early 1960s. Unlike Schurman, the Wagners, Long, and Bentrot not only let the kids have run of the park, but supervised them, taught them climbing skills, and played games with them. A group of West Seattle kids, all "war babies" of about the same age, practically grew up at Camp Long, coming to the park almost daily to find adventure, hang out in the woods, and play games, including "rock tag." The rules were the same on the rock as on the playground: one climber was "it" and chased the other climbers up, over, and around the rock until he or she was able to tag someone, who became "it" and continued the game. The entire rock was in play, including the boulders, North Tower, and the Needle. Surprisingly, despite the sometimes reckless speed climbing involved in trying to tag or avoid being tagged, nobody was seriously injured.

The kids played other games, too, including kick the can, red rover, and flashlight tag. They also played what they called the "Man

Game," which involved several feats of derring-do including climbing the flag pole to the top, jumping across a wide section of the pond, and swinging from one tree to another. One of the boys decided one day to dive off a rock into the pond; he came up with a bloody nose, and none of them tried it again.

Rock tag was a popular game on Monitor Rock
among scouts and neighborhood kids.

Long and Bentrot also taught the neighborhood boys how to belay, rappel, and climb, and enlisted them to help during climbing instruction sessions with Boy Scouts on the Glacier. One day, having nothing better to do, Long took a group of the neighborhood boys for a climb of Mount Si.

During the late 1960s and early 1970s, as the outdoor craze grew and climbing became more of a mainstream activity, unaffiliated rock climbers could often be found climbing on Schurman Rock. Visitors to the rock were required to sign in for many years, and some did, but many did not. Thankfully, the sign-in policy was not heavily enforced, and for the most part visitors who did sign in were not turned away even if they did not belong to an approved climbing group or program. (I myself climbed on Schurman Rock many times in the 1970s and early 1980s, and dutifully signed in, unaware that Camp Long was not open for public use; thankfully, no one ever stopped me.) Once Camp Long was opened to the public, unsupervised use of the rock grew rapidly. Before, kids were subject to watchful adult supervision and instruction while climbing on the rock (if not outright chased off by Clark Schurman); after, hordes of unsupervised children visiting the park scampered all over it, a tradition that continues to this day.

Rappelling down Monitor Rock, 1947.
Photo: Camp Long collection.

There is no way to estimate just how many climbers, young and old, beginner and expert, have climbed on Schurman Rock. Clark Schurman boasted that as of 1947, more than 500,000 rappelling descents of the rock had been made by youngsters without incident. Certainly, thousands of kids—supervised and unsupervised—climb the rock every year, far fewer than when Schurman was running Scouts up and down the rock apparently by the thousands, but still a large number because, by design, there are easy routes to the top that inspire kids of all ages to climb to the top every day.

A Mountaineers class on Schurman Rock, 1977.
Photo: Camp Long collection.

Schurman Rock is a few days shy of eighty years old as of this publication, and although it is aging well, it is aging. Given that it has stood for what is going on eight decades, aside from a few rocks that have fallen out and gone missing, Schurman Rock might seem to be a permanent fixture. However, it has had some structural issues over the years that have threatened its continued viability. The rock had a major addition installed between 1939 and 1941. Early photographs show a broad chimney on the southeast corner of the rock; there is a photo in Fred Beckey's book, *Challenge of the North Cascades*, that shows a young Beckey climbing up the chimney. However, photographs taken in 1941 show that the chimney had been walled in by what is now the Southeast Buttress or "Nose." One supposes this corner of the rock had started to crack and threatened to collapse due to the load of the overhanging wall being insufficiently supported by the underlying structure, and the buttress was added in an effort to shore up the structure and prevent rocks from flaking off or the entire wall from avalanching down.

Park Ranger Tim Fields leads a climbing program on
Schurman Rock, 1984. Photo: Camp Long collection.

By the mid-1980s, erosion on the south and east side of the hill was threatening to undermine the rock's foundation. In a concerted effort led by the Mountaineers Foundation, which provided funding for materials and supplies, and donations by Seattle Steel, Alki Lumber, and Stoneway Concrete, with 833 volunteer hours donated to the project, a retaining wall was planned and built to shore up the hillside. The rock was closed to climbing during the project, which lasted from 1986 to early 1987. After the retaining wall was built and other maintenance performed, and a pea-gravel base was installed, Schurman Rock was reopened on March 18, 1987, which then-Mayor Charles Royer proclaimed as "Schurman Rock Day."

Despite the repairs and maintenance work completed in 1987, by the early 1990s, cracks again began to appear in the rock, especially on the southeast side where the earlier work had been done. The new cracks raised concerns and were monitored, but no repair work was performed right away. But after a winter of record-setting rain in 1999, the cracks grew worse; the rock was finally deemed unsafe, and closed to climbing. A chain-link fence was installed to keep climbers out that remained in place for a few years. (The fence didn't stop climbers, of course, but it and the threat of the rock falling apart certainly bridled their enthusiasm for climbing on the rock.)

One source attributed the new damage to the fact that Schurman Rock had been built over an old stump (visible behind Clark Schurman's knee in the photo on page 16); after so many years encased in rock and concrete, the stump had rotted away, leaving a section of the wall unsupported that had started to cave in. Another theory was that settling following the 1987 renovation had caused the new cracks to appear. Whatever the cause, the cracks in the rock were puzzling, and dangerous. Due to budget cuts and lack of funds, the Parks Department did not have any immediate plans to repair or restore the rock, which created a real risk that the rock might be irrevocably damaged and perhaps even permanently closed and torn down. Thankfully, several generous donors of funds and materials (commemorated on a plaque just west of the rock and a list posted in the nearby kiosk) came forward and contributed the $90,000 needed to repair the rock. After a four-year closure, the rock's footing was stabilized and the cracks were repaired. Schurman Rock, as good as new if not better, was finally reopened in the summer of 2003.

Overall, the rock seems to be holding up well since the most-recent restoration, but it could use periodic maintenance and further restoration. A rock occasionally comes loose and needs to be reinforced or reattached, and some of the old concrete in between rocks is disintegrating here and there and could use patching. Perhaps some of the rocks that have fallen out over the years and gone missing might even be replaced during future restoration efforts. Still, the rock is in no apparent danger of falling down any time soon. One can still climb on rocks set in place under Clark Schurman's guidance eighty years ago—perhaps set in place by Schurman himself—and, with periodic maintenance and restoration work, should be able to continue to do so for decades to come.

At work during the 1986-87 restoration project.
Photo: Camp Long collection.

Compared to indoor climbing gyms, Schurman Rock isn't much of a climbing wall, yet despite its shortcomings, it has always been and remains a great place for beginning climbers to learn the ropes, so to speak. The rock is often tied up with day campers and youth groups learning how to climb, especially during the summer months when day- and week-long youth camps are in session. It is still where hundreds if not thousands of kids each year experience climbing for the first time.

Prior to completion of the University of Washington's Practice Rock in 1976, Schurman Rock was, by default, the most popular bouldering wall in Seattle aside from campus buildings and freeway overpass expansion joint cracks; local rock climbers would come out semi-regularly to hang out, throw a Frisbee, and do some boulder problems. The Mountaineers conducted basic climbing course training at Camp Long for many years, and could be relied upon to tie up the rock all weekend a few times a year. There were lights installed during the 1970s and early 1980s, that allowed night climbing, but they are gone, just like the Mountaineers, who built their own modern climbing wall in 2008 at Magnusson Park in North Seattle. After that, the Mountaineers rarely visited Camp Long except to use the Challenge Course—a high-ropes course completed in 2011 that is frequently used for team-building and leadership training—and to run occasional youth camps on the climbing rock.

Use holds carefully; they can break off! Like any other masonry wall, Schurman Rock needs occasional maintenance work.

There's talk of possibly building an additional climbing wall at Camp Long, one that includes friction slabs, cracks, maybe even an overhang, to round out the park's climbing practice facility and perhaps create a more comprehensive outdoor climbing center south of downtown Seattle. Schurman Rock could even be modified slightly to create "cracks" for jamming and safe lead-climbing practice; it might seem sacrilegious to alter the rock, but Clark Schurman intended his rock to provide training for every aspect of mountaineering. Given that an entire buttress was added to the rock after its original construction, a modest alteration of the rock to make it better serve its intended purpose doesn't seem too outrageous.

Of course, during the past three decades climbing gyms have lured the vast majority of beginning climbers indoors. As a result of this and the construction of the Mountaineers' climbing wall, Schurman Rock has become much less utilized than it used to be. In fact, on some days, the sense of solitude at the rock can be overwhelming unless you count the company of resident hummingbirds, crows, woodpeckers, and occasional passing barred owls and bald eagles as companionship. But on other days, you might run into a handful of other boulderers, a pack of unsupervised kids swarming all over the rock, a nanny belaying her charges up a chimney, a crew practicing high-angle rescue techniques on one of the steeper walls, or a dozen kids roped up, helmets on, climbing all over the rock under adult supervision. Occasionally, a world-class boulderer or local climbing legend makes a pilgrimage to Schurman Rock to find out what this old rock is all about, or to reminisce.

If you happen to come out to the rock some afternoon, hang around for a while. You never know who else might show up.

2.

CLARK SCHURMAN: THE MAN AND HIS MOUNTAIN

Last campfires never die. And you and I
On separate ways to life's December,
Will always dream by this last fire
And have this mountain to remember.

–Clark Schurman

CLARK SCHURMAN IS AN ENIGMATIC CHARACTER, a widower who left his only surviving child with relatives and moved across the country alone following his wife's death at the end of World War I; a Scoutmaster who tore badges off the uniforms of disobedient Scouts who was nevertheless revered by them; a brusque, military-style leader who insisted on dedication, discipline, and doing things "the right way," who also wrote moving mountain-themed poetry; an advertising man who wrapped himself in his two passions—Scouting and mountaineering—and who devoted much of his life to his duties as Scoutmaster, instructing boys in the ways of the wilderness, leading them to the summits of mountains, and preparing them to be self-sufficient in life; a man who loved the mountains of the Pacific Northwest most of all, who shared his love with others through guidance, mentorship, poetry, painting, and an artificial climbing wall he built on a hill in an urban wilderness camp where generations have learned to climb and experience the outdoors.

Clark Schurman self-portrait, oil on canvas, c. 1941.
Photo: Camp Long collection.

Clark Elbert Schurman was born in Beloit, Wisconsin on August 6, 1882 to Lemuel Hooper Schurman (1843-1924) and Sarah Kate Doolittle (1854-1925), who had three children: Clark, Bryce Lorin Schurman (1884-1965), and Blanche Miriam Schurman (1886-1956). Schurman's father was originally a photographer during the era of daguerreotypes and tintypes; the family later moved to Fort Madison, Iowa, then to Julesburg, Colorado, where Lemuel had a boot and shoe store; later, the family moved back to Beloit, then to Avon, Wisconsin, then to Rockford, Illinois, where they ran a grocery store in the mid-1890's, then back to Beloit again where they opened a dry goods store where Schurman worked as a teen. Lemuel resumed photography work before moving to Chicago in 1905; Lemuel and Sarah divorced in 1907, and Lemuel later moved to Pasadena, California in 1920, where he died four years later. Sarah died in Chicago, Illinois in 1925.

Clark Schurman, c. 1885.
Photo: Camp Long collection.

Schurman married Alma Florence Bentley in 1908 in Beloit, Wisconsin, and the couple soon moved to Grand Rapids, Michigan, where Schurman opened his own advertising firm, Schurman Advertising Service, Inc., in or about 1910. According to ad copy placed in the *Grand Rapids Progress* in June 1914, Schurman had for four years written all of the advertising for St. John's Table Co. of Cadillac, Michigan, "which in that time has doubled the number of its dealers and more than doubled its total sales." "Can you beat the 1914 job in 1915?" another ad asked. "You can by getting Clark Schurman on the job to perfect your firm's Goodwill." The *Graphic Arts* (Vol. 6, 1914) ran an article by Schurman extolling the virtues of the Schurman Advertising Service's second man, Walter J. Peterson. Schurman's glowing, somewhat hyperbolic description of Peterson, an illustrator at the firm, seems to have been a nearly perfect description of Schurman himself:

> A versatile ease in the range of his subjects bespeaks
> more than the artist in him... Virility of conception and
> execution characterize everything he does, and are
> perhaps an equal product of an artistic ideal and some
> inborn quality of mind which suggests the maximum
> of effort, always.... [H]e is possessed of an admirable
> calmness that might imperil the spontaneity of one less
> intensely alive.

The apparent success of Schurman's advertising firm, or at least of his effective self-promotion, led to an offer to join a Detroit printing company as an advertising manager and graphic designer, which Schurman accepted. Schurman later took a job as a Boy Scout executive, and served as Scoutmaster for Detroit Troop 13. Schurman was drafted into the Army in 1918, at the end of World War I, but was not deployed. Alma died during the post-war influenza epidemic of 1918. Their son, Robert (known as Bobby to the family), born in 1909, had died in 1910 on his first birthday; their daughter, Ruth, born in 1910, was sent by Schurman to live with relatives in Chicago after her mother's death.

Schurman apparently remained in contact with his daughter, but rarely visited. He nominally published a marriage announcement for

Ruth and her fiancé, Norris L. Brookens, in the Chicago Tribune in 1937. Both Ruth and Norris attended the University of Chicago, where they met; after graduating, Ruth remained connected with the university's Oriental Institute; Norris entered medical school in the fall of 1937 and became a doctor; he later became a founding member of the Board of Regents of the University of Illinois Springfield. They were married on August 28, 1937, and had six children, five daughters and a son they named Clark Schurman Brookens. Norris died in 1969; the Norris L. Brookens Library at the University of Illinois Springfield was created in 1975. Ruth died in 1998 in Urbana, Illinois.

Alma Florence Bentley and Clark Elbert Schurman, c. 1908.
Photo: Camp Long collection.

Schurman did not meet his grandchildren until he returned to Illinois during the year preceding his death, but they knew him from the paintings he sent them over the years, including a painting of Schurman Rock that hung in his grandson's bedroom for many years, and a painting of Mount Rainier given to his granddaughter, Laura, that she later donated to Camp Long.

After his wife's death, Schurman nearly fully immersed himself in Scouting. In 1919, he joined the National Council of Boy Scouts and moved from Detroit to New York City. He was appointed as Editor of *Scouting* magazine the same year. Schurman traveled to the first World Scouting Jamboree held in London from July 30 to August 8, 1920, as Assistant Scout Executive for the American International Jamboree delegation, which included 301 "jamboreeteers" from troops all over the country. Following the Jamboree, Schurman moved across the continent, to Seattle, Washington, where he devoted himself to his new duties as Scoutmaster of Troop 65 on Queen Anne Hill, a post he held from 1921 to 1944.

In 1937, Schurman was appointed as director of an urban wilderness camp project in West Seattle that later became Camp Long. Schurman designed the camp, including the artificial climbing wall, "Monitor Rock," that was constructed in 1938-39. Schurman served as Chief Climbing Guide at Mount Rainier National Park from 1938-41, which earned him the nickname "Chief." Schurman lived in Seattle until 1954, when he moved back to Illinois. He did not remarry. Clark Schurman died at Urbana, Illinois in January 1955 at the age of 72. In 1957, Monitor Rock was renamed Schurman Rock in Clark Schurman's memory.

Schurman served as a Scout leader in Seattle for more than twenty years, taught mountaineering and outdoor skills to hundreds if not thousands of Scouts, and led his Scouts on annual climbing and trail-building trips throughout the Cascade and Olympic ranges. Although Schurman is mostly remembered as one of the founders and the original Director of Camp Long, Chief Climbing Guide at Mount Rainier from, and as the creator of Schurman Rock, the first artificial climbing wall in the world, he was a man of many talents—a poet and an artist, a man with a sensitive soul, as well as a respected community leader and, after moving to Seattle, a mountaineer. Like innumerable transplants before him, Schurman immediately fell in love with the mountains, and soon combined his passions, devoting the rest of his life to climbing, teaching boys how to climb "the right way," and writing poetry about and painting the mountains he so loved.

Schurman appears to have been the consummate Scout leader, who seemed to bridge the early division in the Boy Scouts of

America between the "ax-men" and "typewriter-men." He was deeply involved in Scouting's bureaucracy and management, yet he was a skilled outdoorsman who taught his Scouts to be self-reliant outdoor pioneers, within a structure of strict discipline. In addition to serving as Editor of *Scouting* magazine, he was a frequent contributor to *Boy's Life*, penning numerous letters to the editor and articles extolling the virtues of Scouting and his Troop's accomplishments, yet he was dedicated to training his Scouts in wilderness skills and took them on extended trail-building and mountaineering trips. In some respects, he was a petty bureaucrat in an autocratic corporate organization, but was also an outdoor expert who typified the "backbone of the [Scouting] program." Schurman wasn't one of the "civic club men" who favored exhibitionism; he was an outdoor expert who promoted self-reliance and building character through roughing it outdoors.

Schurman formed Scout Troop 65 in 1920, soon after arriving in Seattle. Troop 65 soon enlisted 300 boys despite Schurman's rigorous admission requirements that focused on dedication, discipline, and commitment. So dedicated was Schurman to his Scouting duties that he also at times served as Scoutmaster of Seattle Troops 214 and 280, in addition to serving as a temporary Scoutmaster for Troop 125, and was in Juneau, Alaska for four weeks during 1921 to start a Scout troop there despite having just formed Troop 65.

Troop 65 had only one Scoutmaster in its entire history: Clark Schurman, who was described by one of his former Scouts as "an inspirational genius of many talents" who had "decided to devote his life to training young men in the skills of campcraft, mountaineering and growing up able to do just about anything that came along." Troop 65 was one of the most well-trained troops in the region, beating out other local troops in eleven out of twelve jamboree contests one year. This was no doubt in part because Schurman had developed a wilderness camp in the woods of Maple Creek in the Wedgwood neighborhood of north Seattle, which had wooden platforms for pitching tents, an outdoor cookout area, and scaffolding in the trees for climbing practice; but most likely because of Schurman's strict discipline and insistence on doing things "the right way."

Clark Schurman upon his return from the World Scouting
Jamboree, 1920. Photo: Camp Long collection.

The Troop eventually gave up the exhibitionism of jamboree
competitions for more civic-minded projects, especially trail building
in Mount Rainier National Park. Under Schurman's leadership,
Troop 65's Scouts were highly active in the mountains, especially at
Mount Rainier. According to National Park Service annual reports, in
1926, "under the leadership of Mr. Clark Schurman," Troop 65's

Scouts constructed a 0.9-mile trail connecting the Ipsut Pass Trail to Eunice Lake in Mount Rainier National Park; in 1928, Troop 65 was building a foot trail over Knapsack Pass; in 1930, they constructed a 1.5-mile trail section linking Klapatche Park with St. Andrews Park, "donating their services and providing their own tools." Each of these trail sections remains in use today. Most of Schurman's Scouts achieved Eagle rank; some of them went on to become climbing guides at Mount Rainier. Scouts from Schurman's troop have been cited as "monumental in establishing a number of climbing routes on the mountain."

Schurman significantly influenced the lives of many of his Scouts, who credited him with guiding them not only in the mountains, but also in their lives. Schurman has been described as being a "forceful presence" in the lives of his Scouts and as a climbing instructor and leader. Dee Molenaar, author of *The Challenge of Rainier*, a member of Troop 65 who went on to become a Rainier guide under Schurman, described Schurman as "an intense, brusque little man with the military way and mustache of General Pershing, [who] had a soul highly sensitive to the beauties of the mountain and to the dreams of youth." Schurman may have had a highly sensitive soul when it came to mountains and his Scouts, but he was quite strict, and disciplined the boys who violated the rules by cutting the Scout emblems off their shirts, even reportedly slapping a boy once, something he immediately regretted and did not repeat.

A former Scout, recalling Schurman's disciplinary tactics, acknowledged that modern parents would not allow that level of discipline today, but felt Schurman, for the most part, exhibited exemplary patience in dealing with large groups of boys, especially when taking them out into the mountains for sometimes weeks at a time. "To the boys of Troop 65 he was always 'Mr. Schurman,'" recalled George Sundborg in a 1986 article. "The Scoutmaster knew only one way to do things—the right way." Schurman, a strict disciplinarian according to Sundborg, was still "a generous leader," and his Scouts "admired and followed him without question."

Stuart Ferguson, a neighborhood boy who grew up next door to Camp Long, remembers Schurman's strict demeanor. "He used to chase us kids out of the park," Ferguson recalled. "Camp Long was for organized groups only back then. He was really strict about that, and wouldn't let us play in the park. We were afraid of him." But Ferguson also remembers Schurman's softer side. "My father died when I was nine," he recalls. "Clark Schurman was walking past me on the sidewalk one day, and I told him my dad had just died. He sort of walked past me without saying anything, but the next day he came to my house and gave me a book, *On to Oregon!* It was his way of connecting with me, I guess, to let me know things would be okay."

When Schurman wasn't leading Scouts in trail building or other projects, he was apt to be leading them to the top of a mountain. Every year, Schurman led climbs up Mounts Rainier, Adams, and St. Helens, usually accompanied by Scouts—lots of them, sometimes 50 to 100 on a given climb. Over the years, under Schurman's leadership, the Scouts of Troop 65 climbed to the summits of most of the major peaks of the Cascades and Olympics, earning them acknowledgement from *Boys' Life* magazine as "a Troop doing things in a big way." One of his Scouts recalled that these climbs weren't risky, or didn't seem so, even for a pack of boys, because Schurman had "trained the kids; they knew how to act in the mountains."

Schurman believed that wilderness training was just as important as other life skills being taught to children. "Children are taught how to swim and how to give artificial resuscitation," he told a reporter in 1947. "I think it's just as important that they learn the use of ropes. Suppose a group of youngsters are on a hike, someone wanders off to pick a wild flower, tumbles down a cliff and can't get up. There's a towline available in the trunk of a nearby car, say. But what good is it if someone doesn't know how to use it correctly."

Of course, wilderness training was more important for his Scouts than your average child, since he was leading them on to rocks and glaciers and to the summits of mountains including 14,410-foot-high Mount Rainier. Schurman boasted that there were no accidents or injuries on any of these climbs. A Scout fell into a crevasse on one climb, recalled one of the boys, but was quickly extricated and the climb went on. Clearly, Schurman taught and commanded his troops well.

.day 16, 1926

THE END OF THE TRAIL

Lake Eunice and Mt. Tolmie in Rainier National Park, pictured here, will be opened by a new trail to be cut by Seattle Boy Scouts. The route will be from Wonderland Trail at Ipsut Pass. This photograph of Scouts at the lake's picturesque shore was made by C. E. Schurman, Scoutmaster of Troop 65.

A 1926 news clip commemorating Troop 65's work on the Eunice Lake trail. Photo by Clark Schurman, Camp Long collection.

Schurman's Scouting activities and trips to the mountains invariably led to interaction with The Mountaineers, one of the Pacific Northwest's longest-established outdoor clubs. Schurman joined The Mountaineers in 1936, and also joined the American Alpine Club. Within a year he was contributing illustrations and poems to the *Mountaineer* journal and had been installed as Club Room Window Display custodian; by 1939 he was on the Editorial Board. Schurman was soon leading climbing instruction courses and climbs in addition to his Scouting activities. At the time, the Mountaineers taught and practiced climbing on a large erratic boulder, Big Rock (later called Wedgwood Rock), located on farmland located a few miles north of the University of Washington campus. Scouts also learned to climb on Wedgwood Rock, taught by Wolf Bauer, a German-born climber and Scout leader, along with Schurman and others. Although a large boulder, some 19-feet high and 80 feet around, Wedgwood Rock had limitations; it could only be climbed via a few routes, and only a few climbers could be engaged in climbing or rope-work at a given time. This was not a problem for the Scouts, since they had a wooden climbing structure at Camp Stanley in north Seattle, and also practiced climbing on city infrastructure such as bridges and retaining walls to hone their rope-handling skills in preparation for climbs in the mountains.

No doubt inspired at least in part by Wedgwood Rock's shortcomings, Schurman envisioned a man-made boulder that could be climbed on all sides that would provide a place for many young climbers to safely learn and practice their mountaineering skills on progressively more-difficult problems. Schurman already had a working model of a climbing training wall, the wooden "cliff" at Troop 65's Camp Stanley, consisting of scaffolding tied to fir trees which he described as a "useful mountaineering gym" that had been used to teach safe climbing techniques to Scouts and other invited guests since 1929. The Camp Stanley wall had its limitations, too, so Schurman continued dreaming of building a more all-around climbing practice rock someday when the chance arose.

Clark Schurman "making out menus," Mount Rainier, 1931.
Photo: Camp Long collection.

The chance arose in 1937, when Schurman became involved in the development of a new kind of park in West Seattle. Teaming up with William G. Long, a juvenile court judge, Ben Evans, director of the Seattle Park Board, and Archie Phelps, a Seattle Park Board member, Schurman helped to turn 68 acres of what had once been part of Puget Mill's timber holdings that was at that time an undeveloped corner of the new West Seattle golf course into an urban wilderness camp, where Scouts and other youth groups could learn outdoor skills. The park provided Schurman with the perfect place to fulfill his vision. During his planning of the project, he researched the idea of a climbing rock and soon began pitching the idea of building a climbing rock at the camp, even building a clay model of his proposed rock to help sell the concept to the Park Board. It worked. Schurman's design was approved and a site was selected, a bare hill on the south side of Camp Long, an area populated by long grass, low brush, several stumps, and a small granite boulder, an ideal location as far as Schurman was concerned because the hill offered an unobstructed view of Mount Rainier to the south, a view he hoped would inspire young climbers to climb higher, both literally and figuratively.

Rocks and boulders to build the climbing wall were appropriated by Judge Long and Archie Phelps, along with nearly all of the other materials used to build park infrastructure, through their "snaffling" and "benevolent larceny." The rocks were stacked up and cemented together boulder by boulder by WPA laborers, under Schurman's close direction and to his exacting specifications. Such was Sherman's attention to detail and insistence that every stone be placed just so, that the WPA workers building the rock thought they were dealing with a "mad-man."

Construction of Schurman's rock began in 1938 and was completed in 1939. Even before it was completed, Schurman had already written an article about "Monitor Rock" for the 1938 *Mountaineer* journal, enthusiastically describing how the rock was envisioned, designed, built, and used. Schurman's article even included a rough guide to twenty-two individual routes and training exercises—"short bits" as he called them—including one problem, "Needle by lariat," that apparently involved lassoing the top of a pinnacle and climbing the rope. According to Schurman, well before the rock was completed, kids were already scampering up it in droves, especially a big kid named Clark Schurman, who stood proudly by as workers set the final stone atop the rock, then bivouacked overnight on the summit following his ceremonious "first ascent."

In 1938, Schurman was invited by the Mount Rainier concessionaire to operate its guiding operation on The Mountain. He accepted, and served as Chief Climbing Guide on Mount Rainier for three years. Schurman's former Scouts recalled him as a "devoted leader"; some of his guides on Mount Rainier remembered "The Chief" differently. Dee Molenaar noted Schurman's "military manner and appearance" and style of leadership; according to Molenaar, Schurman ran a "...disciplined regime, characterized by a 'by-the-numbers' operation of the Guide House..." Chief Schurman reminded Molenaar of General John Pershing, known as a strict, disciplinary military commander. "Several of Schurman's guides were recruited from his Seattle Scout Troop 65," Molenaar recalled in a 2006 article about his guiding days on Rainier, "and they were accustomed to addressing him as 'Mr. Schurman,' and responding with 'Yes, Sir' and 'No, Sir' to his requests in the Guide House."

One writer suggested that, based on Molenaar's description, Schurman sounded like "an old-school hard-ass." This hard-ass approach didn't go over well with some of the other more liberal Rainier guides, who were neither accustomed nor attentive to such autocratic leadership, but overall Schurman was well regarded and his Scouts and guides, including Molenaar, had almost uniformly fond memories of him. To Molenaar, who had come up through Schurman's ranks as a Scout, was urged to attend college by Schurman and study art, and was later invited to become a guide on Mount Rainier, Schurman commanded and deserved respect.

Schurman had long wished that a shelter be built at the base of Steamboat Prow on Mount Rainier's popular Emmons Glacier climbing route. Camp Muir had a shelter, and Schurman thought the popular north-side route also deserved a shelter. This goal was not achieved by Schurman during his lifetime. However, after Schurman's death, his former Scouts banded together to raise money and obtain approval for the project as a memorial to their former Scoutmaster. They sold some of Schurman's paintings and donated money to fund the project, then set to work obtaining and carrying building materials up the mountain.

Clark Schurman with some of his paintings, early 1950s.
Photo: Camp Long collection

Attempts to use horses and a tundra tractor to haul materials failed, so volunteers, including members of The Mountaineers and Boy Scouts, had to carry the materials themselves, including 83 metal plates that weighed between 34 and 40 pounds each, step by step up to the 9,500-foot level of Mount Rainier. Fortunately, cement, sand, and gravel for the foundation were dropped by airplane, saving the volunteers a lot more tiring work. The volunteers poured the foundation, bolted the plates into a horseshoe-shaped frame, and cemented native stone to the outside to create the shelter Schurman had wished for. The shelter took three years to build; started in 1958, it was finished in 1961. The shelter was used as a climber's hut for many years, then as an emergency shelter only, and most recently as a ranger station. Countless Mount Rainier climbers spent a more-or-less comfortable night there over several decades before public use was discontinued.

Despite his drill-sergeant reputation, Schurman had a creative mind and artistic talent. He was a commercial artist by trade, having worked in advertising and graphic design in Michigan before he became involved with the Boy Scouts of America, and continued in that trade after, attending the Pacific Car & Foundry Advertising Conference in 1936. Through his involvement with Scouting, Schurman was introduced to and soon fell in love with the mountains of the Pacific Northwest; he began to write mountain-themed poetry and draw and paint his favorite mountains. Molenaar, a painter, mapmaker, and author himself, recalled that Schurman was "a natural-born artist and he loved mountains." By most accounts, Schurman was constantly sketching.

From 1937 to 1939, Schurman contributed articles, poetry, and illustrations to the *Mountaineer* journal, where his "love of the mountains, talent and creativity … shone through." His essay, "A Mountaineer's Sketch Book," was published in 1939; it featured Schurman's hand-drawn illustrations of seventy-one peaks of the Cascade and Olympic mountains, accompanied by an introductory essay full of Schurman's typically playful prose.

A *mountain* is a hill that is bigger than you think or the sketch shows. A *sketch* is a poetically licensed diagram of one's own mountain, made when it seems probable that the viewers will never have a chance to check up. A *summit* is that portion of a mountain that cannot be reached by lunchtime. A *camera* is an expense that looks an exaggeration right in the eye and says "Really?" *Fog* is a beautiful cloud that has gotten personal. Its best use is to prevent everyone from having to wait for the photographer.

Schurman was a prolific painter, especially later in his life. One of his neighbors recalls his home, an attic loft in the Magnolia neighborhood of Seattle, being filled with paintings of mountains. He sold some of his paintings, but gave many of them away to friends and family members.

Schurman's poems and drawings can still be found in old Mountaineers journals; several of his paintings are hanging inside the Camp Long lodge. One of his favorite poems is inscribed on a bronze placard hanging next to the door of the Camp Schurman ranger hut:

> Into a cloud sea far below,
> I lonely watched the red sun go.
> Then turning, miracle of glad surprise,
> Enchanted saw the full moon rise.

The plaque and poem are lovely reminders of Clark Schurman, but the hut is no longer used as a shelter for climbers as Schurman had envisioned. Given its accessibility and greater use, Schurman Rock is perhaps a more important and lasting legacy for the greater climbing community. After all, Schurman designed the rock himself, lobbied for its construction, and oversaw the project with exacting detail. It was built to teach climbing to youth, and is still used for that purpose today. Thousands of climbers of all ages have learned and practiced climbing on the rock over the past eighty years—rappelling, belaying, and above all how to climb safely, "the right way," as Schurman intended it.

If you look carefully, you can envision Clark Schurman, a short, serious-minded 47-year-old man in 1938, in his shirtsleeves and fedora hat, watching intently and proudly as the final stone was lowered and cemented into place atop his "mountain," then excitedly settling down for his overnight bivouac, watching the sun set over the hill to the west, gazing south to watch the alpenglow fade on distant Mount Rainier.

When you climb at Schurman Rock, remember that every rock is where it is because Schurman insisted that it be there, to be used for the very purpose for which you are using it. If you think about it, think of Clark Schurman, and say thank you.

Mountaineers climbing practice on Monitor Rock, 1947.
Photo by Bob and Ira Spring, courtesy of The Mountaineers.

3.

"MONITOR ROCK"
By CLARK E. SCHURMAN

The full text of Clark Schurman's article, "Monitor Rock," From The Mountaineer, Volume Thirty-One, Number 1, December 15, 1938, pp. 32-35, is reprinted here, with the kind permission of The Mountaineers.

NOT ON EXISTING MAPS, but approximately at Longitude 122° 22' West and Latitude 47° 30' 45" North, is Monitor Rock; elevation, unofficially, 333 feet. It was my good fortune to be in the party making the first ascent, and to be allowed to name the Rock. Moreover, thinking I was young and tough, I tried a just-clothes bivouac, tied to a piton on top. Sleep? What is your guess?

At one stage this rock was a clay model. I was the man in the way when the masons were laying the topmost rock—which explains the first ascent part. The night out was just an old man's folly. Before the rock was a clay model it was a wooden "cliff" at Troop 65's Camp Stanley; part of a useful mountaineering gym of dirt crevasses and balancing devices. Here in one year alone, it entertained 1,200 guests from other invited organizations. Here for nine years it taught "safing" with a rope. And it helped divide the valley sheep from the mountain goats, long before the Scoutmaster had to guess who should join in our long summer treks to the very high mountains. The Park Department knew of these things and brought many committees to study them. Hence the clay model, and then the Rock.

The city is building a close-in camp for the use, in rotation, of all the juvenile character-building agencies that use camping programs. It is a camp on a two-cent school carfare. It includes about 68 acres, near 35th Avenue Southwest, between West Alaska and West Brandon Streets. Its inspiration lies in the snowcapped skylines of the Cascades and Olympics, rather than in the sports page headlines-there is no provision for any conventional games. But twenty-seven minutes from down-town the Scouts may pitch their tents, and welcome, on safe, drained, and eventually shaded terraces; or if it is the week of one of the girls' programs, 150 Camp Fire Girls, Girl Reserves, or Girl Scouts can be accommodated in ten mountain-named cabins.

Features are a forest theatre, miles of wooded trails, a fire-island in a pool, to which all test fires and bean-hole cooking will be confined; measured pace trail, large campfire circles, and a hillside laid out for "wide" games popular with "Y" boys and Scouts, flag raids, treasure and man-hunts. A large parade ground is to accommodate camporals or convention tentage, but not citified athletic games.

In this setting has been placed a beginner's climbing boulder, man-made. And there will soon be built a section of glacial icefall, offering an approximation of ice travel for the training of parties in helping safeguard each other with rope.

The thesaurus offers quite a paragraph of words meaning novice or beginner. One good one is "tyro". Another "abecedarian"—rather a mouthful to teach kids. In the group is "monitor", which the dictionary says means, "One who warns or advises; a pupil selected to instruct or oversee others, usually younger ones; a caution, warning". So this name was chosen for what the clay model stood.

The rest of the prescription was contradictory: a boulder to teach as many rock-climbing skills as might be built into one mass within a given budget, and yet, that would be as safe for an unsupervised group of wandering small boys as their own dooryards.

MONITOR ROCK, Seattle's new climbing boulder for juvenile instruction. (1) Roping over gradual start, and one of the vertical places. (2) Practicing Prusik self-rescue as if in crevasse. (3) Layback, also useful face in, as crack. (4) Rehearsing rope drill to pass bulge above West ledge, with anchor under jutting point below. A place to practice roped falls.

As to the first, there is a chance to teach more than a score of special skills on a rock mass 20 by 30 by 23 feet high, above its base. All the hazards are within nine to eleven feet of kindly earth. There are safe and easy routes all over the boulder, and scores of untutored lads have swarmed over it without a sign of trouble. They dash up the north ramp or stairway and inhale deeply and say, "Huh, I'm UP." Then proceed to greater difficulties by the hour. In spite of this, an expert by ignoring all the gift-holds and working on the smooth faces in the chimneys, and on the wrinkles and "discolorations" elsewhere, can have fun, and find some chance to instruct others.

Here are a score of short bits for demonstration or practice or theory: 1, *A cheval.* 2, Crack. 3, Layback (see cut No. 3). 4, Shoulder-stand to eleven-foot finger traverse. 5, Finger traverse. 6, Same as ledge. 7, Same with piton in use (cut No. 4). 8, Same, for practicing falls. 9, Thirty-inch chimney. 10, Chockstone, passable without help. 11, Chockstone, treated as impassable without rope. 12, Southwest column. 13, Southwest corner. 14, Twenty-five-inch chimney between Needle and Rock. 15, Roping-down place for beginners (cut No. 1). 16, Same vertical (three such). 17, Same, overhanging (two such). 18, Needle, ignoring the safety steps built for novices. 19, Needle by lariat. 20, Overhang for Prusik-loop rescue practice (cut No. 2), or with help, for rescue by two alternately unweighted lines. 21, Face climbs past cooning place on east (three good routes). 22, Cooning place via broad chimney.

With the rock, however small, to help visualize instruction, something can be done in teaching climbing by eye before starting; climbing down before going too far, to memorize the retreat; rhythm, or at least the gradual flow from hold to stance instead of jerky procedure ; correct body positions, hand and foot positions, in a great many situations, (there are more than 130 holds on the main rock); roped party routines and communication: and for those most timid, there is a chance to extend the protection of an upper belay, while teaching all the correct belays on any of five points of three types.

Then there are some valuable land-drills. There are fifty boulders in a mass for constant rhythmic running, surefootedness and familiarity with the slopes at which traction or adhesion is possible in different footwear. Monitor Rock and its adjoining "glacier" may or may not have enough interest to serve the Club's own Climbers' Classes, a few evenings each spring . . . regardless of that, they can serve younger generations, if enough Mountaineers offer their services as instructors, to the organizations whose leaders want technical assistance. All twelve organizations that helped work out the general camp plan, have asked for Mountaineer Climbing Class help when the grass-roots can stand traffic and the camp can be opened to general use. If it seems something to which to invite our own new members also, so much the better.

We catch some days of marvelous clarity, after storms, when Rainier, at this distance, seems more sublime than close on its slopes. Monitor Rock is humble. I hope there is no effrontery in what has been done . . . it has been located on a ridge, the trees behind cleared away, and its best corner oriented to make photographs on these clear days, with Rainier on the horizon. If you are there on such a day, and can drape the Rock and the Needle with your pupils, in correct stances, and can photograph all this, you will be catching with the camera something I know has been in the heart of the man whose energy has made this camp possible. Ben Evans, of the Park Department, has for more than twenty years been thinking of useful things with fun in them for all Seattle kids . . . the city ski area—70 miles from town—is one of them, but they are legion.

The Rock can be no better than the traditions of safety and the quality of understanding set up by us, as coaches. What these traditions will be, five years from now, as to safety and common sense, as to mountain appreciation opposed to personal exhibitionism, will be determined mainly by our Club. If this Rock gets off to a wholesome start, under expert climbers who rise to its possibilities, Mr. Evans' effort will be well rewarded.

"In this setting has been placed a beginner's climbing boulder, man-made."

4.

SHORT BITS:
SCHURMAN ROCK STORIES

SCHURMAN ROCK is not only a climbing rock. It is a gathering place, a magnet for wandering children, curious adventurers, and aspiring climbers of all ages. This book, then, cannot be only about Schurman Rock; it must also be about the people who climb it—all kinds of people, and how they discover it, what they experience, and what they take away from that experience

Who climbs on Schurman Rock? What is their experience? What does it mean to them? Over the past several years, I have probably climbed on Schurman Rock more than any other person. In fact, I am sure of it, because I have come here nearly every day, early in the morning or late afternoon, before work or after, for a quick lunch break or an entire afternoon stolen away from the office, to spend a few minutes or a few hours climbing up and down and around the rock. I've become intimately familiar with nearly every hold on the rock, every gift hold, wrinkle, and discoloration. For the most part, I have had the rock to myself, but every day someone new shows up, a couple of kids with their grandpa, a young couple on a walk with their child or dog, a pack of unsupervised kids on a field day at the park, a group of supervised kids learning the ropes, a teenager trying out his new rock shoes, a retiree thinking of getting back into climbing now that he finally has the time, an old friend who hasn't shown up here in thirty years, and more.

Here are some stories about the people who I've encountered while climbing on the rock over the past several years, presented as a sort of "day in the life" of Schurman Rock. There's a new story every day.

They open the park gates at eight o'clock sharp. Today, I'm there at 8:05 a.m. to get in a morning bouldering session on Schurman Rock. It's usually quiet in the morning. Unless there are campers in the cabins, there's nobody else in the park except an occasional dog walker or retired couple out for an early stroll, who might say hello as they pass, or say nothing. Even when there are campers, they are busy with morning rituals: dressing, eating breakfast, packing to go.

It's quiet this morning as I walk from the parking lot to the rock. I hear a few voices at one of the cabins, kids laughing somewhere in the distance. A brown rabbit is nibbling grass beside the parking lot, ears up, keeping a wary eye on me. A squirrel hops down the trail and climbs the back side of a Douglas fir tree. A jay scolds me from a hemlock limb farther down the trail. A wren darts into the safety of the salal bushes, tail flicking as I pass. Some mornings I see an osprey flying overhead, a fish grasped in its talons; a bald eagle soaring high overhead or perched in a tall tree; a barred owl floating silently from tree to tree. With all the wildlife, I come out onto the Parade Ground expecting to see Bambi frolicking among the clover. It's that kind of morning: quiet, just me and the fauna, perfect for a little climbing on the rock.

And then it isn't. As I come across the field, I see a half-dozen kids cavorting on top of the rock, and hear the familiar crunching of footsteps on gravel below accompanied by unrestrained laughter, which means more kids are playing around the base of the rock. If it was the weekend, it would mean a group of kids had commandeered the rock and might be having any number of misadventures on it: races to the top, stick fights, rock fights, trying to push each other off, what have you. But it's a weekday, which usually means a youth group is in the park for a climbing session. Either way, it's an annoyance. At best, I'm going to have to share the rock with a bunch of unruly kids. At worst, the rock will be closed to the public. Still, I've driven all this way, and am determined to get in a bouldering session, kids or no kids.

Sure enough, there's a dozen or more unsupervised kids horsing around on the rock, exemplified by a trio of boys are scooping up handfuls of gravel and throwing it at each other from various places on and around the rock.

"Please don't throw gravel," I tell them as politely as possible while I'm changing into my rock shoes. "There are other people here."

"Yeah," says one of the girls, who acts like she's in charge.

The boys stop for a minute, but are at it again as soon as I am out of sight.

"Seriously," I say as I climb up over the top edge of the rock, startling them. "The gravel's there for safety reasons, and I don't appreciate getting hit by rocks while I'm climbing. And you get gravel all over the rock, which makes it unsafe up here. Somebody could slip on the loose rocks and fall off."

"Yeah, knock it off," two of the girls tell them in unison.

The three boys, who look like they might be brothers, begrudgingly knock it off. It's clear that the anti-rock-throwing sentiment is rising now; they are outnumbered. They scramble down and wander off to do their mischief elsewhere.

"Did you just climb up that wall?" asks a tall girl who's wearing a Mickey Mouse t-shirt.

"I did," I say. "Aren't there any adults here with you?"

I take a survey of the dozen or so pre-teens scampering around the rock. Girls outnumber the boys 3-1 now that the troublemakers are gone.

"They're at the cabins," says another girl, looking at me over the top of her red-framed glasses.

"They told us to go play while they cleaned up after breakfast," explains another girl, who's sporting black-and-maroon corn rows.

"There are safe and easy routes all over the boulder."

"Are you all together then?"

"Our school group is camping out here," she tells me. "We're from Oregon."

I go about my business, climbing laps up and down my usual circuit of boulder problems. A few of the kids are astonished as I climb the various walls with a minimum of holds, and pepper me with remarkably intelligent questions:

"Does the chalk help your grip?" ("Can I try some?")

"Do those shoes make it easier?"

"Do you always climb without a rope?"

"Have you ever climbed El Capitan?"

A small group of kids is collectively working out the easiest route up the tower and, then, the way down, which is a three-foot step across from the tower to a ledge on the main rock, fifteen feet off the deck, a scary proposition. A girl in a bright purple pullover has made it to the top first; she contemplates the step-across move but balks at the exposure. A boy in space-cadet sunglasses is coming up right behind her, and a girl wearing a bright pink hat is closing in fast. Meanwhile, another girl wearing a light blue headband is stemming up between the tower and the main wall, attacking the problem directly. She reaches the top and steps across easily. The others, having seen it done, quickly follow.

The group reconvenes at the southeast corner of the rock, a stone-studded buttress that is not quite as steep as the other walls. The girls lead the way again, the girl in the pink hat climbing up one side of the buttress, purple pullover girl up the other. The boy in the red shirt and the space cadet are right behind them. After a few aborted attempts, they are on top and looking for another route to try.

"What should we climb now?" a boy wearing a red shirt asks me.
"I can't really tell you what you should climb, you know," I tell him. "If I do, and you fall and get hurt, your parents will sue me."

"No they won't," he assures me.

"Are your parents even here," I ask.

"My mom is," he says.

"Does she know you're over here climbing on the rock?"

"No."

"Hmm," I say. "Well, some kids seem to manage to climb up the crack on the other side of the rock. I'm not saying you should climb it, just that I've seen some kids climb it."

"Thanks!" he says. "Come on you guys!"

Meanwhile, two of the girls in the group have been quietly working out the moves up the steepest side of the rock. They've removed their shoes and socks and are climbing barefoot to get a better grip on the slick holds. They aren't talking with anybody, not even each other. Each is in her own world, in the zone, completely focused on climbing the wall. The girl with the pageboy haircut sees me watching her and almost glares at me, as if I'm interrupting her flow. The other, an Asian girl with a pony tail, seems oblivious to my presence. She's obsessed with finding a route up the steepest part of the wall. She tries one way, then another, grabbing this hold and that, probing for a line of weakness. Finding none, she climbs down and surveys the wall, then tries again.

"If you can get to that big hold to your right, the rest is pretty straightforward," I suggest.

"Oh," is all she says. Like I said, she's all business.

She moves to the right, reaches up to the big hold, repositions her feet, and hangs there momentarily. She's now on the steepest, blankest part of the wall; except for the big hold she's latched onto with both hands, there are only a few thin handholds. Still, a big smile comes over her face. She knows she's won. From here, she can get her feet on a couple of big footholds and make a long reach past the smaller holds to a higher hold that is the key to climbing the wall. She grabs it easily, pulls up, and is soon on top. The other girl works out a different route up the wall. Both bound down the easy ledges and are back for another try. On the other side of the rock, the gang of five is engaged in a mass assault on the crack.

That's when the adults show up.

"Did you know they were here?" I ask a man in his late thirties, the first grown-up on the scene, who is standing there with his arms folded, looking stern yet seemingly amused, proud even. He's one of the teachers.

"No," he says. "Have they been causing any trouble?"

"Not at all," I assure him. "They've been very well behaved. I don't think I've ever seen a group of kids on the rock as polite as these kids.

"They're really into climbing," I add. "It's great that you expose them to this kind of thing."

The boy in the red shirt walks by and says hi like I'm his new best friend. He starts climbing the tower again behind purple pullover girl, who is in the lead once more. More adults arrive. They don't seem quite as amused as the teacher.

"Oh, my gosh," one woman exclaims upon seeing the kids climbing all over the rock. "What are you *doing* up there?"

"I'm climbing, Mom," the boy in the red shirt says cheerfully.

"That doesn't look safe," she says fretfully, almost to herself.

"It's great that the kids have been left alone to do this," I tell her. "They're really an adventuresome bunch. Does their school encourage this sort of thing?"

"Yes," she says, without a hint of enthusiasm.

*"...as safe for an unsupervised group of wandering small boys
as their own dooryards."*

"It's probably better that the parents don't know what's going on sometimes."

"Yeah. It's making me nervous. I have to bite my tongue."

"It's good that nobody's telling them to get down," I assure her. "I think it's important to let kids test their limits. They've been pretty safe so far. They're amazingly self-reliant, and they're really into it."

"I can't watch," she says, then adds before she walks away, "Steven, you be careful."

"Okay, Mom," he says right before he does the step-across move for the third time.

"Five more minutes," the teacher announces. He's feeling the vibe from the parents; it's time to call them down. "Then come back to the cabins. It's almost time to leave."

"Aww," comes a collective groan from the kids. They each climb the rock once more, and then run to the cabins and they're gone.

It's quiet now. And although I had come hoping to have the rock to myself, I kind of miss the company.

○

RORY AND CHASE SEE THE ROCK from across the field and head off at a dead tear for it, leaving their grandfather in their dust.

"The rock!" yells Rory, who is five years old, as he runs.

"The rock!" yells Chase, who is almost four.

"You kids wait for me," Grandpa says, but they aren't waiting, they're running full blast down the grassy hill and across the clover-infested field. They arrive at the rock out of breath but excited.

"I'm going to climb the rock!" Rory yells, and he does just that, scampering up the big, easy ledges to the top where he pumps his fists triumphantly. He's already on top before Chase arrives.

Chase hesitates on the way up. The rocks are slick, and it's a little scary being so high off the ground.

"...scores of untutored lads have swarmed over it without a sign of trouble."

"Come on, Chase!" Rory says. "You can do it."

Chase tries another way. He has to crawl onto one of the boulders with hands and knees, but makes it to the top unscathed.

"This is the biggest rock in the world!" Rory shouts from the top.

"It's not a rock," says Chase. "It's a bunch of rocks stacked up and cemented together."

"You kids get down from there," Grandpa says as he huffs up the path toward the rock.

"It's easy, Grandpa," says Rory. "You should climb the rock, too."

"Yeah, Grandpa," Chase says. "Climb the rock with us!"

"I don't think so," Grandpa says. "You should come down before you fall and hurt yourselves."

"Okay," Rory says. He scampers down quickly. Chase starts down, but stops at the first steep bit.

"I'm scared," he says. "Help me, Grandpa."

"I'll help you," Grandpa says, and he climbs slowly up the big, step-like ledges to reach Chase, who has gone back to the upper ledge. "It's neat up here, isn't it Grandpa."

"It's kind of high up," Grandpa says. "Come on now. Sit on your butt and slide down. I'll be right here to keep you from falling."

Chase complies and they are both soon back on terra firma.

"I did it!" Chase says.

"Good job," Grandpa says. "Where's your brother?"

Rory, meanwhile, has run around to the other side of the rock, out of sight of Grandpa, and is already halfway up the tower, a steeper climb up a 15-foot high pinnacle. It's easy going, on big holds and ledges, but ten feet up he hesitates. Being this high up is unnerving. He's not sure he should keep going, but feels compelled to finish the climb before Grandpa calls him down. He tries one way, then retreats and tries another way, which leads him to an intermediate ledge just below the top.

"Get down right now!" Grandpa scolds as he comes around the corner and sees what's going on. "I told you to not to do that."

"But it's fun, Grandpa," Rory says. "I'm almost to the top."

"Well, never mind that," Grandpa says. "Climb down now. You're scaring me."

"Okay, Grandpa," Rory says. He climbs down dutifully but a little dejected, knowing he was one move away from the top.

"Can we come back again someday?" Rory asks as they hike down the path back to the meadow. He's already planning his next assault on the tower.

"Yeah, can we?" Chase asks. "That was fun."

"We'll see," Grandpa says. "Maybe your dad can bring you next time."

☙

COMING TO SCHURMAN ROCK AFTER 10 A.M. on a summer weekday is a crapshoot. The park officially opens at ten, and that's when they start their day-camp programs. Some days, no programs are scheduled on the rock; other days, they're running climbing courses all day. By coming later in the morning, I'm rolling the dice, hoping to come out with a seven or eleven. Today, it's snake eyes.

Yohann Hanley is one of Camp Long's outdoor program directors. Yohann's a gentle, bearded, teddy bear of a guy. He exudes patience and kindness but has a commanding voice, the perfect combination for someone who works with kids every day. This morning, to my disappointment, he's instructing a group of third graders from a local elementary school who are having a party to

76

celebrate the end of the school year. Ropes are dangling from two sides of the rock. The west side of the rock is rope free and potentially open for climbing, but the sign says CLIMBING ROCK CLOSED and they mean it. More than once I have been politely instructed by a 15-year-old girl—one of the teen outdoor instructors that Camp Long's programs produce every year—to get off the rock because it's closed for an organized group session. The first time, I tried to talk her out of it.

"I'll just climb over here," I said. "I won't get in your way. You won't even see me."

"I'm sorry," she told me gently but firmly, like a teacher instructing a preschooler who's asked to stay up and play during nap time, "but you can't climb on the rock right now. We'll be done at four o'clock," she added. "You can come back then."

Another day, I tried to plead my case with Yohann. He told me a story. "Kai Lightner came to Schurman Rock one day," he began. "You know who Kai Lightner is, right?"

Kai Lightner is a teenage rock climbing phenomenon from the East Coast, an African-American kid with arms like an albatross, who discovered climbing at age six and now climbs 5.14 and wins a lot of competitions. If it wasn't for climbing, he'd probably be just another nerdy teenager trying to figure out what to do with himself. Instead, he's one of the rising stars of the sport.

"So," Yohann continues, explaining to me why I can't climb on the rock today, "Kai comes to the rock one day with a photographer, and they're setting up to do a photo shoot. We're just about to start a class and I tell them that the rock will be closed in fifteen minutes. 'Is it okay if we climb over on this side?' Kai asked. 'No, sorry,' I told him. 'We have to close the whole rock.' 'But,' the photographer says, 'this is Kai Lightner. Do you know who *Kai Lightner* is?' 'I'm sorry,' I told her. 'It's great that he's come to climb on the rock, but we have to close the rock when we have a class. It's for liability reasons. If it was me, I'd let you, but I have to follow the rules. You have fifteen minutes before we start.' The photographer was pissed, but Kai was like, 'Okay, I understand.' I felt bad, but…"

"...a boulder to teach as many rock-climbing skills as might be built into one mass within a given budget..."

(Photo by Isabel Herbruger, Camp Long collection.)

"I promise I won't trip over your ropes," I assure Yohann, pretending I didn't understand the point of his story, hoping he'll make an exception for me just this once.

"I'd let you, but we're teaching the kids how to climb safely," Yohann says firmly but gently, just as his protégé has always done. "It sets a bad example for the kids to have somebody soloing around on the rock while we're doing a class."

"Okay," I say. "I understand."

"I'm glad," he says. "Last week a guy came out with his son to climb on the rock. He got really mad when I wouldn't let them climb. He started swearing at me right in front of the kids."

"No worries," I say. "I'll just climb on the north tower then. It's not closed, right?"

"Nope," Yohann says. "Go for it."

Although the main rock is closed when there's a class, the north tower is open. The north tower is a mini-Schurman Rock, a stack of boulders and bowling ball-sized rocks cemented together. It's not quite ten feet high on one side and maybe thirty feet around at its base, not much of a climbing rock compared to the main wall. It is usually only climbed by children who have been talked down from the main rock by their anxious parents, who assume that the north tower is not as dangerous to climb because it's not as high as the main rock. I'm not so sure, unless landing on boulders from ten feet up is safer than landing on flat, loose gravel. In any case, a lot of kids experience climbing for the first time on the north tower and get up and down it without incident, just like on the main rock. It's also a place where this big kid tries to amuse himself when he, too, is not allowed to climb on the big rock.

As I sit down atop the tower to change into my rock shoes, I can see and hear what's going on over on the main rock. Yohann and his assistant have the kids lined up against the railing and are instructing them on the basics: selecting and putting on a harness, how to wear a helmet, how to tie in, how belaying works, the importance of signals, keeping in balance while lowering off, how not to be scared. Yohann explains everything thoroughly but engagingly. He makes eye contact; he smiles; the kids eat it up and pay close attention. It's like the first day of Little League practice, but with ropes and harnesses instead of bats and balls, presumably more dangerous than baseball but, after coaching youth baseball for many years, I'm not so sure. I've seen a lot more kids hurt on the ball field than on the climbing rock. The kids who climb roped up, tied in, on belay, wearing helmets, are keeping it super safe. It's the rogue kids you worry about, who climb the rock without ropes, without adult supervision. You'd think they would get hurt more often, but contrary to conventional wisdom, they don't seem to.

There's a theory that the kids who are climbing unsupervised without safety equipment are more cognizant of the risk than those who are tied in, and manage that risk more effectively. Or maybe it's because of the rock's design; on three sides, there are ledges partway up the wall that allow kids to avoid climbing too high off the ground; also, the holds get bigger near the top, making the climbing easier, lessening the chance of falling off; and there's loose gravel on the ground to cushion your fall should you slip off. I've taken quite a few surprise falls off the rock over the years because of a foot slipping off a hold or messing up a dynamic move, and have come away unharmed. Maybe I'm lucky. The few kids I've seen limping off after climbing on the rock have usually decided that jumping is the best way to get down. It isn't.

"Does anybody know why we wear helmets?" Yohann asks the attentive schoolkids.

"To protect our brains?" a girl says, unsure if she has the right answer.

"That's right," Yohann says. "Do you know why we want to protect our brains?"

No one is brave enough to answer. After a moment of awkward silence, Yohann tells them.

"Our brains are like eggs," he says. "We don't want to scramble them.

"This area here," he continues, pointing to his forehead, "controls our personality. If you scramble this part of the eggs, you may go up the wall Timmy, but come back down Tommy. And this area here," pointing to the back of his skull, "controls our vision. If we scramble these eggs, we won't be able to see. So we need to be sure to put the helmet on like this, so it protects our whole brain, so we don't scramble our eggs, okay? So everybody get a helmet and we'll put them on."

They select their helmets, then their harnesses, and go through the whole litany of safety steps, which takes twenty minutes. The kids are restless; they want to start climbing. Meanwhile, I have my rock shoes on and have started climbing. The tower's so short, and isn't very steep on any side, so it isn't much to work with. I can do some one-handed problems, or climb using only the index fingers of each hand, or pinkies-only even. Today, I devote my session to climbing without using my hands. I've worked out a circuit of no-hands problems on the tower, up two of the three walls as well as a traverse around the entire tower, walking my way from hold to hold like a tightrope walker.

"When we climb," Yohann is telling the kids, "we always maintain three points of contact. Do you know why?"

Some of the kids look over at me hiking up the tower without using my hands, puzzled looks on their faces. Clearly, that guy isn't following the rules.

I'm in an experimental mood today. Although I've tried, I haven't managed to climb the north side of the tower without grabbing hold to keep my balance on the last move. I've worked out a route in theory; it involves stepping onto a small hold no bigger than my big toe with my left foot, then stepping up to a downward-sloping rock with my right, from where I must commit myself and step all the way to the top with my left foot and then do a massive one-legged press to stand up. This works in theory, but any number of things could go wrong. Mostly, I'm concerned that my right foot will skid off just as I'm committing to the step to the top, which would likely result in some sort of dental surgery, maybe a broken nose or fractured skull, too, as I smack my face into the upper ledge then topple backwards onto the boulders. I give it a halfhearted try, but wimp out and grab hold with my hands at the last minute. I circle back and try again. I get up to the hard move again easily, and have to decide: am I going to do this or not?

To my relief, my feet stay on and I am standing on top. I want to do it again, but don't. Not today with the kids watching. I don't want to set a bad example, after all. It would be bad form to fall and hurt myself on a six-foot-high wall in front of a bunch of third graders who are trying to learn how to climb safely. So I try something else. I get the idea to see if I can eliminate some holds. As if it isn't enough that I'm climbing without using my hands, now I'm trying to reduce the number of rocks I use as footholds. On one side I manage to get up the tower using just three rocks as footholds. Then I get it down to two. Can it be done with one rock? Impossible, it seems, but there are some patches of concrete in between the rocks that can serve as tenuous footholds. I give them a try and they work. One rock: check. Can it be done with no rocks?

So there I am, climbing on the kid's rock, trying to climb it without using my hands or any of the rocks. Even Yohann is looking over now, wondering what the heck I'm doing.

☁

"OH, LOOK. A CLIMBING ROCK."

A young mother is out for a stroll through the park with her children. Her four-year-old son is running ahead, already making a beeline for the rock; her two-year-old daughter is ambling along, staying close to Mom.

"Be careful, Matthew," she says as her son starts scrambling up the staircase of boulders toward the summit. "Make sure your feet are on good holds. Stay in balance."

"All the hazards are within nine to eleven feet of kindly earth."

He does as he's told, climbing upright, slowly, making sure his feet are set before climbing up to the next ledge. In a minute, he's at the top.

"Look at me, Mom! I did it!"

"Yes, you did it. That was very good," she tells him. "Wait there while we climb up to join you. Stay back from the edge please. I don't want you to fall off."

"I won't," Matthew says, sitting down against the highest rock to wait.

Mother and daughter ascend the rock. The mom lets the daughter do the climbing, occasionally offering a steadying hand and some reassurance. The little girl crawls from ledge to ledge with her mother right behind her. They arrive on top together.

"You did it, Maddie!" mom says when they reach the top. "I'm so proud of you!"

The little girl is beaming.

"Okay, let's climb down. Matthew, why don't you go first so we aren't in your way?"

"Okay, Mom."

Matthew climbs down carefully, and is soon on the ground. He can't wait for his mom and sister, and has soon clambered up the north tower.

"Look, Mom," he shouts. "I climbed this rock, too!"

"That's great," she says. She's guiding Maddie's foot down to a ledge, helping and reassuring as before but still allowing Maddie to do all of the climbing herself. They're halfway down the rock. "We'll be right there."

Matthew is already down from the smaller rock and running around the side of the big rock. By the time his mom and sister have reached the ground, he's halfway to the top.

"Where are you, Matthew?"

"I'm up here," he answers, letting go with one hand to wave.

"Look, I'm climbing the steep side!"

"Oh, my," she says. "Do you need help?"

"No, I can do it."

He's ten feet off the ground now and has done the hardest part. He has a hold of two big holds and is in no danger of falling, but the final move is giving him pause. He tries one way, then another, to get his feet up on to a higher ledge, but can't.

"I'm stuck," he says.

"It's okay to use your knees," his mom tells him.

He tries again, bringing a knee up to the ledge, which gives him enough leverage to reach a higher hold and finish the climb.

"Wow," Matthew's mom says. "Good job."

Matthew is smiling wide as he scampers down the easy way.

"That was fun," Mom says to her kids. "There's a pond over there. Should we go over and see the pond?"

"I don't want to go to the stupid pond," Matthew says. "I want to climb on the rock!"

"We'll come back to climb on the rock another time," Mom tells him.

They head off toward the pond, Mom and Maddie out in front, Matthew dragging his feet behind.

"Russell?" I ask, unsure if it is really him.

"Yeah," he says. His voice is unmistakable.

Russell Erickson used to be a fixture on the local rock climbing scene in the 1970s and 1980s, who would pop up at far flung places such as Joshua Tree, Yosemite, Squamish, even Mount Arapiles in Australia. I used to hang out with Russell at the University of Washington Practice Rock back then. Russell was almost always there, in shorts and a t-shirt, climbing in tattered E.B. rock shoes before they came out with sticky rubber. I ran into him a lot at the Index Town Walls, and in Leavenworth, too. He was in Joshua Tree every time I was ever there, and in Yosemite and at Smith Rock, too, living out of a tent or the back of his station wagon for weeks or even months at a time. I could not tell if it was coincidence or if Russell really did spend all of his time traveling and climbing. As far as I could tell, Russell worked for a few months during the winter, then spent the entire spring, summer, and fall traveling and climbing. When he ran out of money, he went back to work; when he'd made enough money, he'd quit and go climbing. He led an enviable lifestyle, one I was never brave enough to fully embrace.

And then Russell all but vanished. For thirty years. Someone would come back from somewhere and say they'd seen Russell, but he was mostly nowhere to be found. He'd dropped off the face of the earth. No phone, no email, no fixed address. Rumor was he was in Australia again, or California. So, it was a complete surprise to find Russell at Schurman Rock of all places, bouldering by himself on a sunny weekday afternoon.

"It is you! Wow, it's been thirty years since I've seen you," I say. "What brings you here."

"I'm visiting my brother," he says. "I've been here for a few weeks."

Same old Russell, I think, but not the same old Russell. It's still Russell, but he's older. A lot of the climbers I grew up with were a few years older than me; when I was sixteen, my mentor, Erik Thixton, was in his twenties. Russell was about Erik's age, which means he might be pushing sixty. Damn! But old or not, it is the same old Russell in spirit, still hanging out at the rock, full of youthful enthusiasm for climbing. Like me.

"I haven't been here since probably the seventies," Russell tells me. "We used to come here to boulder before the U.W. Rock was built. Then when they built the Rock, we stopped coming here. It was too far away."

Russell tells me stories about the old days, about how he and so-and-so used to come out to Schurman Rock from the U. District on their bikes or the bus and climb, play rock tag, work out hard problems. He's working on one of the old problems now, an eliminate problem up the steep side of the detached tower, something a little harder than the main route up the face. Something we both used to be able to climb, but not today. He tries it one way, then another.

"I'll get this," he says. "I used to do it all the time."

"I've got a problem for you," I tell him. "Follow me."

We go around to the back of the rock to work on a contrived traverse I've made up. Like Russell's problem, I last did this one ages ago, but haven't been able to do it lately. I give it a go and fail. Russell gives it a try. Same result.

"This place is so great," he says. "I love this kind of climbing. Just making up problems and working out the moves."

"Yeah," I agree, "it's pretty fun."

"Well, I have to get going," Russell says after we give our problems a few more tries.

"You need a ride?" I ask. I want to hang out longer, but he declines.

"No, I'll walk. It's not far to my brother's house."

"Give me your phone number," I say.

With the rock...something can be done in teaching...roped party routines and communication...

"I don't have a phone."

"Email then."

"I don't have email."

"What's your brother's number?"

"Gosh, I thought I had it written down here," he says, fumbling through some scraps of paper in his wallet, "but I can't find it."

I give Russell my phone number, but I know he's never going to call me. He'll disappear again. This chance meeting at Schurman Rock will probably be the last I ever see of him. I'm just glad we got to spend an hour bouldering together. Just like the old days.

"How hard do you think this is?"

This is me at age fifteen, asking some old guy climbing at Schurman Rock about a boulder problem. I was a scrawny kid then, just learning to climb. The old guy might have been in his sixties, a prototypical old-school climber of the day in his leather mountain boots, army surplus knickers, and wool sweater, tied in with a bowline-on-a-coil while toproping with a thick Goldline rope. This is what real climbers looked like back then. I figured he would know.

The subject of my question was a steep wall on the west side of the detached pinnacle, a seemingly holdless, 15-foot-high vertical wall that I had been trying unsuccessfully to climb for some time. How hard it was, I had no idea. I'd climbed a 5.8 once; this was harder.

"That?" the old guy said, looking up at the wall and rubbing his chin. "That one's pretty hard. I'd say 5.7."

Either he was sandbagging me, or he was completely out of touch. I mean, sure, Fred Beckey's guidebooks were still saying 5.10 was the highest level of difficulty possible when there were routes rated 5.11 and even 5.12 in places like Yosemite and the Shawangunks, but 5.7? This? No way. It was harder than 5.8, for sure. I guessed it must be 5.9.

"How hard to you think this is?"

This is me, forty years later, and I'm still not sure how hard that problem is. I'm asking an old friend, Mark Gunlogson, who's joined me for a bouldering session this afternoon. We used to climb here back in the '70s. We went our separate ways for a while, but have reconnected and meet at the rock sometimes to climb and reminisce. Mostly, we complain about how old we have become and how hard all of the old problems seem now. Like this one.

"I don't know," Mark says after a failed attempt. "What do you think? 5.11?"

"Yeah," I say. "Hard 5.11. Could be 5.12."

"Could be," he says. He tries it again, gets up a move, looks up at the next hold, a fingertip edge in the middle of the face, and jumps down. "I need to get down here more often," he says.

"How hard is this?" It's a fifteen-year-old kid wearing a t-shirt from a local climbing gym who just showed up at the rock one day. He's been trying and failing to climb the problem for a while now.

"I don't know," I say. "Let me give it a try."

I get on the wall and crank through the moves. I have it pretty wired now. Even at my advanced age, I can do the problem nearly every time. For how long, I don't know. Use it or lose it, they say.

"Some old guy once told me it was 5.7," I tell the kid. "What do you think?"

"You mean V7, right?" he asks me.

"Sure, V7, " I say. Whatever that means.

Hans Florine is a curious character. He is best known as a Yosemite climber. More specifically, he is best known for climbing on one cliff in Yosemite: the 3,000-foot-high granite face of El Capitan. But it gets even more specific than that: Florine is best known for climbing one particular route on El Capitan: the *Nose*. Florine has climbed the *Nose* more than 100 times. And as if that is not enough, Florine has held the speed record on the route, on and off, since 1990. In 2012, he and fellow Yosemite climber Alex Honnold climbed the *Nose* in 2 hours, 23 minutes, 46 seconds.

If you think Hans Florine is obsessed, you may be right.

Florine was in town one night giving a slide show. He showed photos of his ascents of the *Nose* over the years, talked about his philosophy, his speed records, his obsession. When you meet him, he seems like a laid-back guy. Then he starts talking about the *Nose*, his initial failure, his eventual success, his methodical approach to improving his efficiency, cutting his time on each successive climb, his first one-day ascent, his eventual speed record of 8:06 in 1990 that cut almost 2 hours off the prior record set by Yosemite free-climbing legends John Bachar and Peter Croft, then losing and reclaiming the record six times over the following twenty-two years. When Hans Florine starts talking about the *Nose*, he gets that look in his eyes.

"If somebody broke your record again," somebody in the audience asks, "would you try to beat it."

"I don't know," he says. But you know he's lying. He'd be picking a partner, somebody fast and competent who's climbed the route several times, like Honnold; he'd be working out like a fiend all winter; he'd be making a series of speed ascents the next spring, tuning up for a record attempt; he already has it planned. Then, one day, you'd hear about his new speed record on the *Nose*.

"I think the record can be lowered by about five percent," Florine told us. I did the math. If you knock off five percent of 2:23:46, you get 2:15. For a 3,000-foot-high route, that's 22 feet of vertical climbing per minute.

"...an expert by ignoring all the gift-holds and working on the smooth faces in the chimneys, and on the wrinkles and 'discolorations' elsewhere, can have fun..."

On October 21, 2017, Brad Gobright and Jim Reynolds climbed the *Nose* in 2:19:44, beating Florine and Honnold's record by four minutes. There's room for improvement. I have no doubt Hans Florine, who has now climbed the *Nose* 110 times and counting (a record that will be hard to beat), has already called Alex Honnold.

The day after Florine's show, I am at Schurman Rock, wondering how long it would take me to climb 3,000 feet of rock. Schurman Rock is no El Cap; to do an "El Cap" day—climbing the equivalent "mileage" of an ascent of El Cap—I'll have to improvise. The rock is about 18 feet high; by my calculation, I'd have to climb 84 laps up and down the rock to equal 3,000 feet of climbing. To make it legitimate, I'd have to actually *climb* down the steep walls, not just scramble down the easy way, so I'm actually *climbing* 3,000 feet. I'd also have to top out on each lap and touch the summit block, just to make sure I climbed all 18 feet every time.

The sun has broken through the clouds and it is threatening to become a glorious winter day, but a dark cloud is drifting in from the south, threatening rain. I quickly lace up my rock shoes, tie on my chalk bag, and get to work. In 15 minutes I've climbed 15 laps, a lap a minute, on pace for a 1 hour, 24 minute time. Then rain hits, big splashing raindrops that instantly soak me and every inch of the rock. I keep climbing until the holds get too slick for comfort. You could really get hurt if you fell off in the wrong place. I'm thinking of calling it a day, but the rain softens, the sky brightens, and a nice breeze comes up as the cloud passes and in a few minutes, it's sunny again. The rock dries off fast, and before long I've finished 30 laps in 29 minutes.

I've climbed easy problems so far, but to keep it real, I switch to more difficult problems, picking three problems in the 5.10-5.11 range and climbing them ten times each. I'm not climbing as fast now; the harder problems take longer, and are more strenuous, especially when you climb them back-to-back, nonstop. I'm soon panting like I'm on the third lap of a mile race. I pass the Half Dome mark—56 laps, 2000 feet—in 1:04. So far, so good, but I'm about to come up against the biggest obstacle to my El Cap day: tedium. After an hour of non-stop climbing, I'm getting bored. I'm finding it mentally difficult to want to keep climbing up and down, up and down the 18-foot-high rock. I love climbing on Schurman Rock, you know, but I'm starting to not love this. It's a chore. I have to will myself to keep going.

Schurman Rock isn't a big rock. It's fairly small, so there are only so many problems you can make up before the variations start to seem meaningless and repetitive. Dreadfully repetitive. To climb here often, one must not merely suffer repetition, but embrace it. Unlike a lot of climbers, I don't mind repeating a problem. I prefer it. This was John Gill's approach, and John Bachar's. Not satisfied to have merely "ticked off" a route and say they'd done it, both Gill, the Godfather of modern bouldering, and Bachar, the iconic free-soloist, embraced the spirit of repetition in pursuit of Zen-like perfection of artistic performance on rock. To me, Bachar exemplified this approach; seeing him on his soloing circuit at Joshua Tree in the early 1980s, casually climbing 5.11 and 5.12 routes unroped, was inspiring. I adopted Bachar's approach almost wholeheartedly, and applied it to every climb I did, even down to the boulder problems at Schurman Rock. I have my own circuit here, thirty or so problems that can keep me engaged for a couple of hours climbing at a leisurely pace, day after day after day. But speed climbing is something completely different. It's not meditative; it's not Zen-like. It's go, go, go, as fast as you can, until your body gives up, or your mind, or both.

I pick three more problems, each about 5.9 in difficulty, to finish it off. I climb the first problem ten times, or think I have, but have lost count, so I do a penalty lap just to be sure. Now my feet are starting to hurt, increasing the urge to quit. I climb the second problem ten times, losing count and climbing a penalty lap again. I have blisters on my fingertips now that are starting to tear open. Just four laps to go; each is physically and emotionally painful, but the finish line is in sight. I persevere.

I climb down after lap number 84 and check my time: 1:34. Do I think the new record on the Nose can be beaten? Yes. Do I think Hans Florine will reclaim the record. Yes. Yes, I do.

I'm ready to call it a day, but while I've been climbing, I've been thinking. At the slide show, Florine said he'd climbed the Nose 103 times so far. I'm already up to 84 ascents of Schurman Rock just today. What's another 19 laps?

After I finish lap 103, I'm wondering: how many laps in a mile.

If you think I am obsessed, you may be right.

"Which way is the climbing rock?"

It's a boy's voice. He's been running ahead but has stopped at the intersection of four trails. Even though he's only thirty feet away from the rock, he can't see it; it's hidden behind a bushy redwood tree.

"Just up this trail," his mother answers.

He runs up the trail, the gravel crunching under his rapid steps.

"Here it is," the boy says excitedly. He runs along the base of the rock, looking for an easy way to climb it.

"Wait, Eric," his mother says. She's walking more deliberately behind, carrying a baby girl. Eric stops, looks back at his mom impatiently. He's all energy, ready for action.

"Why don't you try this rock over here?" she says, pointing at a smaller tower on the north end of the structure.

"Okay," Eric says. Whatever. He dashes through the boulders and scampers up the tower, then looks back at the main rock. "Do you think anybody has ever climbed *that* rock?"

Of course, his mother is thinking, but she doesn't want to crush his spirit by telling him the truth, not yet. "I don't know," she says. "What do you think?"

"I don't think so," Eric says. "I'm going to climb it!"

Eric scampers across the boulders and climbs to the top of the rock easily, all the way to the very top.

"...it helped divide the valley sheep from the mountain goats..."

"Look, Mom!" Eric shouts as he stands atop the summit block. "I'm the first person to climb the rock!"

"That's awesome, Eric," she says. "Why don't you come down now so we can go do some other things."

"Okay," Eric says. He starts climbing down the ledges, facing toward the rock. His mother stops him.

"Why don't you turn around and slide down on your bottom?" she says.

"This is fine," he says. "I can do it."

"I think you would have better control and less likely to slip off that way," she says.

"No," Eric says, "this way is better. See?"

"Alright," she says, acquiescing. "Be careful."

Eric makes his way carefully down his way, and arrives safely at the bottom.

"See," he says. "That was easy."

"Good job," his mom says. "Let's go see what's down that trail."

"Okay," Eric says. He runs ahead of his mom, as always, eager to see what's down the trail.

"CAN YOU TELL US WHERE THE CLIMBING ROCK IS?"

It's an odd question coming from woman in her seventies who seems dressed more for a visit with relatives than an outing to a climbing rock. "Clark Schurman used to tell me about his climbing rock," she explains to the front desk staff. "It is such a beautiful day today. We decided to come to find it."

*"And there will soon be built a section of glacial icefall,
offering an approximation of ice travel for the training
of parties in helping safeguard each other with rope."*

(Photo: Isabel Herbruger, Camp Long collection.)

"You knew Clark Schurman?"

"Oh, yes," the woman assured her. "He was my friend."

Nancy Tegman was a young girl when her parents moved to Seattle's Magnolia neighborhood in 1948, next door to the Hertzman family. The Hertzmans had a lodger, one "Mr. Schurman," a balding, well-dressed man in his midsixties, who wore a fedora hat whenever he went outside. "He lived in a room in the attic with a pull-down staircase," Tegman remembers. "I used to sit outside on the steps in front of my house. Mr. Schurman would walk by occasionally and say hello. Then one day he stopped and talked to me."

"Mr. Schurman," looking for a dining companion, invited Tegman to join him for lunch. That led to more trips. "We would go out for Chinese food," she remembers fondly. "He took me on a field trip to a museum to look at artwork. We rode the bus. He didn't like to go out by himself. He wanted company, so he took me along.

"I know it seems kind of strange or inappropriate now," Tegman says, almost seventy years later, "for an older man to be taking a ten-year-old girl out on trips around the city. But he was always very kind. A gentleman. He was a friend to me."

One day while visiting the Hertzmans, Tegman was invited up to Mr. Schurman's room to look at his paintings. "He had paintings of mountains all over the walls of his room," she remembers. "He let me choose one of his small paintings. I still have it," she says proudly. "My parents also bought one of his larger paintings; I have that, too."

Tegman remembers Schurman returning to his daughter's home when he got sick a few years later. "That was the last I saw of him, but I often thought about him.

"Mr. Schurman used to tell me about Camp Long and the climbing rock," she recalls. "So, a couple of years ago, my husband and I drove out to West Seattle to find that rock." With directions from the front desk staff, they found it, up on the hill just as Schurman had described it. "It was very meaningful to me," she says.

"He was so proud of that rock. Finally seeing it brought back some wonderful memories."

$$\mathbb{C}$$

THEY CLOSE THE GATES AT 6 P.M. SHARP, so I know I'm taking a chance in coming to the park after 5 p.m. to get in a quick session before I head home. If I'm not out by six, they'll lock me in. It's happened before. I was able to get myself out of the park that time, but I had to leave my car overnight and walk home. Lesson learned. I keep a close eye on the time.

Although it's close to closing time, the park is surprisingly busy. There are people walking dogs, playing Frisbee on the meadow, jogging on the trails. Nobody's on the rock when I get there, but the people walking by invariably stop and climb the rock before heading on their way. All kinds of people climb the rock on a given day: children, teenagers, young couples, whole families, retired couples, you name it. In the half hour I'm here this evening, a dozen people wander by and climb to the top for the view.

Even though a lot of people stop and climb the rock, it's rare to find another climber here, but tonight I am not alone. An older guy is here, older than me anyway. He's wearing some old-school climbing shoes I've never seen before.

"What brings you here?" I ask, thinking it's a more appropriate line than 'Do you come here often?'

"I just retired," he says proudly. "I'm finally getting paid to do what I want I want to do.

"I used to come here when I was a lot younger," he continues. "I did a lot of climbing back in the sixties and seventies, but then I got married, got a career, and stopped for a long time."

"It happens to the best of us," I say.

"Now that I have some time on my hands," he continues, "I thought I'd try to get back into climbing. This is my first time out in thirty years."

"If this Rock gets off to a wholesome start, under expert climbers who rise to its possibilities, Mr. Evans' effort will be well rewarded."

His story makes me wonder why we quit doing something we love, like climbing, when we get married, start a career, have kids, become an "adult," only to take it up later in life, when we "have time." I did the same thing. During my late teens and early twenties, I lived to climb. Then I met a girl, got married, had a kid, immersed myself in my career, and almost completely disappeared from the climbing scene. Not everyone did this, of course; Fred Beckey didn't do this, but he was an exception. Most of the climbers I knew followed a similar course; they put their climbing gear in a box, stored it in the garage or basement, and let it sit there, unused, all but forgotten until many years later, when the climbing bug bit them again, after their children had grown up, they'd retired, divorced, or their spouse had died, and they took up climbing again because, deep down, it has always been what they really wanted to do. It is as though all of those years of repressing their love of climbing had suddenly bubbled up and boiled over. They found the box of climbing gear stored in the garage one day and made the mistake of opening it and allowing those old longings to rush out with no hope of stuffing them back inside.

So it is that we are here at Schurman Rock this evening, a couple of old guys reliving their youth in the best way they know how, climbing on a little rock in an obscure park at the edge of a little city in a corner of America, reminiscing about the old days, the hard work of getting back into shape, the grief of so many wasted years, the hope of a few more good years before we once again have to quit climbing for reasons we can't very well control.

"When I quit climbing, I assumed I could always pick it up again," he says. "I don't take it for granted now. Just doing something simple like coming out to the rock is a joy. I really appreciate that I can still do this. I don't have forever to do things anymore. I have to make the most of every day."

"This is a perfect place for us old guys to hang out," I say. "It's just us and the rock, no pressure, no egos, no crowds. You can hear the birds, feel the breeze, just enjoy yourself for a little while without worrying about anything."

"I wish I hadn't stopped climbing," he says. "But now I have no excuses. I have nothing better to do!"

I get so wrapped up in our conversation that I forget to look at the time. It's 5:55 p.m.

"Okay, well, great to meet you," I say as I gather up my street shoes and start running for the parking lot.

They are closing the gates behind me as I drive away.

Toproping on the West Column, Schurman Rock.

5.

A CLIMBING GUIDE TO SCHURMAN ROCK

An hour's practice . . . will do more to get your climbing muscles in order than many of the recognized moderate courses. . . . you put in twice as much work and that work is two or three times as difficult. It is extremely hard to convince some climbers of this. They must go off and do something big, and megalomania bears them away captive . . . Nevertheless, if one can do so, one will be more than repaid by bouldering.

–Claude E Benson
British Mountaineering, 1909

Climbing to the top of Schurman Rock is not particularly difficult. Dozens of kids climb it nearly every day. Indeed, the rock wasn't designed with difficulty in mind, but rather safety. It was created to provide a place that kids could learn and practice various climbing techniques in a relatively safe environment under adult supervision. Among the kids who scramble up the rock every day, many are participants in youth climbing programs, experiencing climbing for the first time just as Jim and Lou Whittaker did in 1941: roped up, on belay, learning to climb "the right way" under the supervision and direction of an adult instructor.

For beginning climbers, it is usually challenging enough to climb up one of the steeper walls using any available holds. And for some, that is enough; they are content to have climbed the rock, touched the top, scrambled down or lowered off, and are soon off to other adventures. But for some, this is not enough; once they have mastered the basic technique and climbed the basic routes, they want more. Yet Schurman Rock is just a small pile of rocks cemented together; what more could there be?

The North Tower is a good place to introduce kids
to the sport of bouldering.

There is plenty more. Clark Schurman described twenty-two unique "short bits" in his 1938 *Mountaineer* article, and identified some 130 individual holds that could be used for climbing on the rock. He was off to a good start. There are, in fact, a lot more "short bits" that have been and may yet be contrived on the rock, and many,

many more holds to choose from than Clark Schurman counted. Although Schurman designed his rock for training and practice, he unwittingly created a perfect wall for what would become the sub-sport of climbing known as bouldering, one of the most popular types of climbing in the world today.

Bouldering is the simple activity of climbing on rocks (or their surrogate) close to the ground, where ropes and equipment are not required but may be employed for safety where desired. Bouldering on artificial walls is possibly the most contrived type of climbing there is. It is also one of the most enjoyable. On real rock, you climb whatever is available: a face, a crack, some combination of the two, whatever gets you up the wall. On an artificial climbing wall, as on many natural boulders, you can pick and choose. In fact, much of the fun of bouldering is being able to make up enjoyable or difficult problems using only selected holds to match your skill set or challenge you to improve. In that respect, Schurman Rock provides almost unlimited fun.

Since Schurman Rock is literally a pile of rocks stacked up and cemented together, there is seemingly no limit to the number of potential climbing routes that could be contrived on its various faces. One can enjoy an hour or two of easy bouldering, climbing just the most-obvious "natural" lines—buttresses, arêtes, chimneys, and the faces in between, using all of the holds or picking and choosing, making up routes as one goes. However, there are more than 100 distinct "established" problems on Schurman Rock's various faces and buttresses, not counting a seemingly infinite number of possible variations. Most of the best and hardest problems are elimination problems that climb a given wall with only a limited number of rocks, using or excluding certain "big" rocks, or disallowing certain holds as footholds; indeed, each natural line can yield several contrived problems as hold after hold is eliminated until one is climbing the wall with only three or four holds allowed for hands and feet, often with long reaches or lunges in between. Many of the problems can be climbed using only one hand or the other, or only a particular finger on each hand; a few of them can even be climbed without use of hands at all.

Working out an eliminate traverse on the West Face.

As an example, the Southeast Buttress ("Nose") of Schurman Rock, a relatively low-angle wall composed of dozens of small blocks, is a fairly easy problem if you use any available hold; indeed, kids regularly clamber up this wall despite their parents' admonitions to get down before they hurt themselves. To make it more challenging, a climber might limit the number of rocks allowed as handholds to, say, four rocks for the hands, still allowing all of the rocks for the feet, then reducing the number to three rocks, then two, and finally one rock for the hands. There might be forty possible four-rock variations on this wall, another thirty three-rock combinations, twenty two-rock combinations, and ten one-rock problems. Right there you have one hundred distinct, contrived boulder problems, and you haven't even considered the many possible problems that could be made up limiting the rocks you can use as footholds, let alone one-handed problems, or the possibility that the wall can be climbed without using any rocks for your hands at all. And this is just one section of one wall on the rock. If you start applying this concept to every wall, there are thousands of possible boulder problems that could be made up.

Elimination problems are nothing new at Schurman Rock; even in 1938, Schurman suggested that expert climbers could have fun on the rock by "ignoring all the gift-holds" and using only "smooth faces," "wrinkles," and "discolorations" as holds. He was onto something. This is exactly the kind of fun that has endeared artificial climbing walls to local climbers for decades.

So far, bouldering at Schurman Rock has remained a relatively low-key affair without a lot of importance given to difficulty or ratings. Although there are not a lot of truly difficult boulder problems here, with some focused attention by some talented modern boulderers, some very hard boulder problems could be worked out using the many overlooked "wrinkles" and "discolorations" on every wall.

Even though Schurman Rock doesn't have a lot of impressively hard boulder problems, it is a great place to get in a workout if you live in the south end and don't belong to the West Seattle fitness club (which has an indoor climbing wall), can't make it to the nearest climbing gym regularly (they're so far away!), or don't want to put up with the usually bad Seattle traffic to get there (ugh!). The secret to getting a good workout here, as anywhere, is repetition and "mileage," doing laps up and down or around the rock. If you pick easier problems, you can get in a lot of mileage in a fairly short time. If you pick harder problems, you can get in a really solid workout in a very short time. Assuming, of course, you don't go insane first.

They switch out the holds at climbing gyms fairly often, setting new problems to keep things interesting; at Schurman Rock, it's been the same old thing every day since 1939, which can drive you a little nuts after a while, but it beats doing pull-ups in the basement, and it gets you outside, in touch with real rocks, in the sun and wind and sounds of nature instead of pulling on plastic holds in a sweaty gym, worrying about whether the last guy who climbed a given problem wore his rock shoes into the men's room. Besides, part of the fun of climbing on Schurman Rock is using your imagination and making up a problem that is challenging to you instead of climbing problems a route setter has made up for you.

Of course, it would be an absurd undertaking to try to climb every possible contrived boulder problem on Schurman Rock, and even more absurd to try to include every possible contrived boulder problem on the rock in this guide. To avoid this sort of absurdity, and to keep this book small and manageable, I am including only a few dozen of the most obvious, "natural," historic, and classic boulder problems on each wall. There are many more problems to be worked out on the rock; many have been done, many have not. If the problems included here are not enough for you, use your imagination and make up some "new" problems. There is no shortage of possible contrived boulder problems to keep you entertained for hours, days, even years.

As with real climbing routes, boulder problems are given a name, sometimes after a famous climber of yore (e.g., "The Beckey Route"), sometimes by committee, and sometimes a name made up by a guidebook author to provide a way to more easily identify a given problem. Following this custom, each of the boulder problems included in this guide has been named. In many cases, the name is generic, describing the physical feature being climbed (e.g., "South Column"). However, especially for more-contrived problems, a more fanciful name has usually been assigned (e.g., "Fly or Die"). Where a problem did not already have an established name (i.e., most of the problems since nobody beside Clark Schurman has ever bothered to name them apparently), I have tried to make up route names that reflect the history and environment of the rock and park, especially route names and terminology used by Schurman to describe his original routes on the rock. So, if you're wondering where the name "Needle by Lariat" came from, now you know.

In several bouldering guides of yore, including guides to real boulders and artificial climbing walls alike, the boulder problems have been illustrated by numbering the holds. An early example of this is John Menlove Edwards' 1935 *Guide to the Helyg Boulder*, a "catalogue of sorts" to the many problems on a single boulder in England, which were indeed catalogued by Edwards, with all of the handholds assigned a number and all the footholds assigned a letter, leading to problems described as, for example, "Hands ... 11 to 9, Feet G&H to F&E." A written guide to the Michael Sobell Centre climbing wall in Islington, North London, similarly assigned numbers to each hold and defined problems by listing the numbers of the holds that could be used, in order, for example, "28, 28, 31, 20." In their 1992 guidebook to the University of Washington Practice Rock, Scotty Hopkins and Erik Wolfe went so far as to name the key holds on each wall, e.g. "sharkfin," "flag," "tooth," "black pebble of death"— names that had been bestowed by climbers over the years—so that some of the problems could be described by naming the holds used, such as "lunge from the sharkfin to the flag using only the black pebble of death as a foothold."

Since Schurman Rock is composed of a number of individual rocks, a numbering system could be used here to catalog every conceivable problem. And some of the individual rocks have been given names, e.g., "beak," "flake," "pinch hold," "egg," to help identify certain problems or holds. However, using a numbering system would have its challenges, especially at Schurman Rock, which has hundreds if not thousands of individual rocks, some of which have several distinct holds on them. I am sure such a useful numeric-based guide to Schurman Rock could be created, but am not sure such a guide would be practical. I will leave it to someone else to do so should the need arise.

Rather than numbers, boulder problems in this guide are described in plain English, with "topos"—photographic illustrations with overlain route lines and details. Each problem will be described so as to provide its location, key identifying features, the "rules" imposed on the problem (such as which rocks are allowed or disallowed as hand- and footholds), and any safety considerations where there is a clear objective hazard. The route descriptions will not go into excessive hold-by-hold, move-by-move detail such as J. P. Rogers did in his description of the Overhang on Puddingstone in his "Boulder Valley" article published in the 1916 Fell & Rock Climbing Club journal:

> The Overhang is a pure gymnastic stunt and consists in jumping for a projecting rock 8'6" from the ground and swinging up until it is under one's left armpit. Then with a sloping right foothold to assist, it is possible to draw one's-self up by means of a right handhold until a knee can be placed on the tongue. From here the rest is easy.

There won't be any of this sort of "left armpit" nonsense in this guide, nor precise inch-by-inch measurements. Here, such a problem might be described with less detail, and might leave key details out so you can figure out the problem for yourself, such as: "A two rock problem using the projecting rock on the left and a higher hold on the right; if you can't reach the first rock, you will have to improvise something."

First ascent information is omitted because, really, who knows (or cares) who was the first to climb these problems? People have been climbing on Schurman Rock—and making up "new" boulder problems—for eighty years now. I have made up dozens of boulder problems on the rock over the past thirty-plus years, but don't assume I was the first to climb any of them. Let's just assume Clark Schurman, Wolf Bauer, Ome Daiber, Dee Molenaar, Fred and Helmy Beckey, and Jim and Lou Whittaker climbed all of the best boulder problems at Schurman Rock long before you or I were born or even knew the rock existed.

Even so, it's fun to make up new problems, even if they probably aren't really new. If they are new to you and provide you with an engaging challenge, that's all that really matters.

The "Dime-Edge Traverse," a crimpy eliminate problem.

BOULDERING TECHNIQUES

Most of the bouldering on Schurman Rock consists of climbing what used to be called "cling holds"—face holds that you cling to with your hands and fingers. Modern climbers more often use the terms "open" or "crimp" to describe how a hold is gripped with the hand. In an "open" grip, the hand or fingers are cupped or curled over the rock surface; a "crimp" involves locking down on a thin hold with the fingertips, with the knuckles bent inward to maximize downward force on the fingers. It is useful to know that an open grip is more natural and less likely to cause injury than crimping, but thin holds may require crimping. If you do a lot of crimping on small holds, your fingers will start to ache much sooner than if you use an open grip. If you persist in crimping through the pain, you may suffer tendon or ligament damage, chronic joint pain or arthritis, or possible fractures. If your fingers start hurting during a crimp-intensive bouldering session, it's time to work on some less-crimpy problems or call it a day.

Rock holds can be used in a variety of ways to create any number of unique problems. You can pull down on the top edges; do side-pulls on the side edges; undercling on the bottom edges; or any combination of the above. Some problems allow any or all of a given rock to be used; others require that the rocks be used in only a specified way. For example, some problems allow only the side edges of rocks ("side-pulls"); others, only the bottom edges ("underclings"). Some problems don't use any of the edges, but only "features" on the faces of the rocks—the tiny edges and flakes and undulations in the rock itself that might otherwise be overlooked.

You can mantel up onto various rocks and ledges; manteling is downward force with the hands and arms that allows you to bring your feet up onto the same hold as your hands, as if you were climbing up onto a fireplace mantel or kitchen counter.

You may be able to stem your way up a few problems; stemming involves outward counterforce with hands and feet against opposing rocks or walls. As an example, the big chimney on the west side of Schurman Rock is usually climbed with left hand and foot on the left wall and right hand and foot on the right wall, pushing in opposite directions to stay on the rock; this is stemming. There are only a few places on the rock where stemming is feasible. It is a good technique to learn and practice, especially if you plan to go climbing on real rocks or in the mountains.

Some problems require lunging: controlled dynamic moves to reach holds that are just out of reach—or a long way out of reach in some cases. There are several fun problems involving lunging from this to that hold; sometimes lunging is not required but is more fun than doing a static move; sometimes a lunge is the only way to reach a higher hold. Lunging usually violates the "maintain three points of contact at all times" rule, and sometimes lunging requires committing to an irreversible course where failure results in a less-than-desirable, out-of-control fall. Lunging should be done in a controlled manner; no wild leaps into space, as those usually result in a longer fall than you might wish to take when you come up short of the target hold. Lunging can be practiced on holds close to the ground to minimize fall potential; it is wise to practice lunging a lot before you commit to a big lunge way off the deck. Always have a spotter, pad, or use a toprope if you are lunging high off the ground.

There are not really any friction problems at Schurman Rock, although you can use friction technique on the faces of some of the rocks and features, palming a flat or rounded rock face with your hands or smearing with your feet on wrinkles, rough rock, and concrete patches. "Scumming" is a form of friction where you smear or wedge any body part available to assert leverage or maintain affinity with the rock, such as a hip, shoulder, leg, arm, knee, or your face even. Early boulderers maintained friction by laying against the rock in the hope that their clothing would provide sufficient friction to keep them from slipping off; this was the earliest form of scumming. If you are sliding down on your butt, using your "fifth point of suspension" as Clark Schurman called it, you are scumming. Scumming is usually very useful in chimneys and on "no-hands" problems, which usually require a lot of groveling, just without using the hands. Scumming can be helpful to maintain balance where there is a wall or rock to lean against, but is not a very glamorous technique.

To "Gaston" means to use outward counterforce, in the fashion of the famed Alpinist, Gaston Rébuffat as illustrated in his book, *On Rock and Snow*, as if trying to pull a crack apart by pulling outward with both hands. Some cracks and even a few face climbs can be climbed in this manner. Many an enjoyable session has been devoted solely to working out as many Gastoning problems as possible.

This is a brief overview of some bouldering techniques and terminology; there are a lot of other bouldering and climbing terms and techniques that I won't go into here. If you hang around in a climbing gym for a while, you'll probably pick up the lingo fairly quickly. At Schurman Rock, all you're likely to hear is parents yelling "Get down from there before you hurt yourself!"

A one-handed ascent of the West Face.

There are a few places where you can practice leading on Schurman Rock. The cracks can be protected if you use large chocks or camming devices, and the big bolt on the west face offers a convenient protection point for leading a few routes on that wall. As noted elsewhere, the ring bolts on the west side of the Needle are historical relics that should not be used as protection or aid practice as they probably would not hold much more than body weight any longer after eighty years in place. One should not place pitons or use hooks on this rock or any other artificial climbing rock, as they tend to cause irreparable damage. (Jim and Lou Whittaker brought pitons to the rock one day to practice piton placement. "We caught hell for that," Jim recalled.)

THE "RULES" OF BOULDERING

There aren't any particular rules for climbing on Schurman Rock other than "climb at your own risk. " Other than that, it's right there, ready for you to climb on it however you like. As long as you aren't damaging the rock, annoying others, harassing wildlife, or creating an unnecessary safety hazard, pretty much anything goes.

Jim Bridwell, the Godfather of Yosemite rock climbing in the 1970s, once famously said, "There are no rules in climbing." That may be so, but there *are* rules in bouldering—a lot of them, especially on the climbing walls. The rules, such as they are, are imposed to make the climbing more mentally engaging and physically challenging—that is, more fun. Bouldering that requires mental problem solving to work out physically difficult moves is most rewarding, which is why bouldering, once considered mere practice for real climbing, has become such a fast-growing segment of the sport.

Climbing on artificial climbing walls is different than ordinary rock climbing in several respects, one of which is that, in real climbing, successfully climbing a given route means simply climbing from bottom to top using whatever natural features are available to complete the ascent. If there's a crack, you jam it; if there's a ledge, you mantel onto and stand up on it; if there's a face hold, you grab it. There is never, or at least rarely, any impetus to avoid using a bomber jug or not jamming your feet into a crack just to make a real route more difficult. Who would do that?

Some rules of bouldering (and fashion) are definitely being violated here! Photo: Camp Long collection.

But in bouldering and, by extension, climbing on artificial walls, it is not only common but expected that one will try to make a given problem as difficult for oneself as possible by eliminating as many holds as possible. Further, the "rules" of artificial wall climbing codify how a given problem must be climbed to achieve the desired level of difficulty. These rules are usually straightforward but sometimes complicated, depending on which holds and techniques might or might not be allowed for a given problem. The description of each problem in this guide will define the rules for that problem. The rules affect the ratings, which assume you are facing the rock and using every hold available within a given boundary unless restricted under the rules of that problem.

You don't have to follow the rules, of course, and since conventional ratings are not used in this guide, it doesn't matter if you don't; you are free to climb these problems facing away from the rock, with your shoes on the wrong feet, using only your thumbs and big toes, or however you like. If you are a "real" boulderer, of course, you will like to climb them with some rules imposed to make them as engaging and difficult as possible.

In general, if you are climbing a face problem, cracks and arêtes are out of bounds; use only the embedded rocks and concrete features on the specified area of the wall, and avoid grabbing, jamming, or otherwise using cracks and arêtes or reaching around corners unless the problem specifically allows it. Rocks for the feet may be eliminated on some problems, requiring use of only concrete features as footholds, a difficult elimination on most of Schurman Rock since the rocks are stacked pretty tightly together leaving little exposed concrete on most walls.

A more feasible alternative is to use features on the rocks themselves, the little edges, wrinkles, or blank faces of the rocks but not the tops, sides, or bottoms of the rocks. You can define "features only" on Schurman Rock however you wish; however you define it, using features only for hands or feet makes a given problem much more difficult, as the features are usually small, and requires much better technique.

A few problems include or can be done with a sit-down start to eke out one or two additional moves of difficulty, often the most-difficult moves on the problem. Gravel may need to be cleared out to excavate a key foothold on such a problem. Some people love sit-down-start problems; some hate them. If you don't want to do a problem with a sit-down start, don't; you can start standing up and have almost as much fun.

Climbing the North Tower using index fingers only.

The usual bouldering rules concerning crack climbing are almost impossible to implement at Schurman Rock, which has only a couple of cracks to begin with, neither of which can really be climbed using modern crack-climbing technique. It's unfortunate that Clark Schurman didn't include a couple of finger- or hand-size jam cracks in the design, but at the time jamming was a largely unknown technique; the two cracks that were constructed are boot-cracks that can be climbed by layback, a hand-stack or two, or Gaston technique. You could try climbing them with no rocks for the feet, but since the rock is composed almost entirely of rocks, that would be difficult; another alternative is to use "features only" for the feet including the faces of rocks but not their tops or sides. Give the cracks a try one way, then another. If they're too easy, eliminate some holds.

A few problems are or can be "synchronized," where you may use a given hold only once, as a handhold usually, and never again. This usually makes a problem more difficult than if you allowed unlimited use of a given rock or hold. For example, on a four-rock problem, you might use your right hand on the first, rock, left hand on the second, right on the third, and left on the fourth. You can't match hands, switch hands, or use a given rock again as a handhold if you have already used it. Grab it, pull through, and don't touch it again. Or not; synchronizing a problem only makes it more interesting and fun, but you don't have to do it if you don't want to.

An "English" problem allows use of designated holds for both hands and feet, and all other holds are disallowed except concrete features as necessary to make the moves between rocks, unless otherwise specified. There are some English problems that do not allow use of features for the feet, only the specified rocks, which makes more sense at Schurman Rock since there aren't a lot of features to use for the feet. In both cases, you can grab the rocks with your hands and also step on them with your feet, but not any other rocks for either hands and feet. Sounds complicated, doesn't it? If this doesn't make sense to you, you are probably better off; just climb however you like and have fun.

When doing a boulder problem properly, you aren't supposed to touch the ground or use any off-limits holds or other assistance even for balance. Sometimes you may accidentally touch the ground with your foot, or maintain your balance by touching an illegal hold just for a second. Technically, this invalidates your ascent, at least if somebody is watching or you are a purist. Some climbers will disallow an ascent if a spotter merely touches their shirt during the climb, on the theory that the spotter may have inadvertently aided the ascent. Not everyone is so circumspect; some people just climb for the joy of it and don't worry about such trifles.

Specific contrivances and eliminations are detailed in the description of each problem. Some problems are straightforward and require little discussion; others are quite contrived, sometimes too much so to be included here.

Of course, you don't have to follow the "rules"; sometimes it's fun just to climb whatever, however, and just enjoy yourself. In fact, the only rule you should strictly follow is: "have fun." If you aren't having fun, you're doing it wrong.

BOULDER PROBLEM RATINGS

"A need for a rating system has long been recognized by American climbers," wrote the late Fred Beckey in his *Cascade Alpine Guide*, "for simple words such as 'easy,' 'moderate,' and 'difficult' are subject to a variety of interpretations." Since this is climbing guide, using a rating system seems appropriate, even necessary, but which system?

Bouldering ratings are a tricky business, and not an exact science. The original bouldering rating system, the "Gill System" named after its creator, John Gill, has been supplanted by the "V Scale," which is the most-commonly used bouldering rating system in use today. Although I like John Sherman, the creator of the V Scale (which I refer to as the "Sherman Scale"), I dislike his rating system as it, like the Gill System, is somewhat elitist and dismissive of climbers for whom even an entry-level (e.g. "B1" or "V1") problem is too difficult, giving them little more than a feeling of inferiority when they can't even climb the easiest level of bouldering difficulty. Then again, bouldering ratings have to start somewhere, and the Sherman Scale pays homage to the Gill System by starting at approximately the same level of difficulty as an old-school Gill "B1" (around mid-5.10).

Gill, one of the first American climbers to apply gymnastics to short rock climbs as an end unto itself, viewed bouldering as a distinct sport from climbing which started approximately where rock climbing ended difficulty-wise, and intended his rating system to "[challenge] climbers to improve their technical skills to the point they were capable of 'bouldering level' difficulty [B1], although it was not always taken that way." As Gill noted, "Climbers tended to want more instant gratification, a number that would validate their progress or prowess as the case might be, not only to test their technical skills, but also to compare them with the skills of other climbers, to see who was 'better.'"

An existing rating system, the Yosemite Decimal System, provided just such a basis for comparison. When I started climbing in the mid-1970s, the best climbers were climbing 5.12; a few 5.13 routes were rumored to have been climbed, but were somewhat shrouded in mystery and often referred to as being "5.12+" in difficulty; those numbers set a high bar which, like the bar in the high jump or pole vault, ambitious young climbers aspired to clear someday.

So it is with young climbers today; they tend to view each progressively higher rating as a stepping stone in their development into an awesome climber, something to aspire to and achieve as a measure of their impressive skill. This does not happen much at Schurman Rock, of course; here, most climbers are unconcerned with ratings, preferring to simply climb what they can and challenge themselves to climb what they can't, without undue concern for what it is rated—the way it's supposed to be.

With all of this in mind, and with due regard for Fred Beckey's opinion but not feeling especially bound to it, I am not using any of the existing rating systems in this guide. Instead, I'm using a rating system suggested by a local climber from the 1970s, Rick Graham, who believed boulder problems fell into three categories of difficulty: "hard," "harder," and "too hard." Of course, there are a lot of "easy" problems at Schurman Rock, and some "moderate" problems as well, since it was designed for kids and beginning climbers. It's hard to differentiate between a "5.1" and "5.2" route on the YDS scale, and there's no equivalent on the Sherman or Gill scales that makes any sense since only a handful of problems at Schurman Rock would even register on either scale.

"Gee, Pat, was that traverse a V4 or a V5?"
Mountaineers' group outing at Monitor Rock, 1941.
Photo by Bob and Ira Spring, courtesy of The Mountaineers.

Accordingly, despite Beckey's admonition, the "Graham System" will be expanded to include "easy," "moderate," and "difficult"

124

ratings before getting to "hard," above which the Gill system will be used to denote "true" boulder problems of "B1" difficulty and higher.

Under this system, "EASY" will denote problems that most kids will have little trouble climbing with the confidence of a toprope, perhaps up to 5.6 in difficulty. A "MODERATE" problem will be a bit harder, perhaps in the 5.6-5.8 range (a "VB" or "V-Fun" problem under the Sherman scale). Moving up the scale, "DIFFICULT" problems will be 5.9-5.10 on the YDS scale (about "V0" to "V1"). A "HARD" problem could be anywhere from hard 5.10 to hard 5.11 (generally in the "V2" to "V3" range). Above that, a "B1" problem will probably be around 5.12 in difficulty or even a little harder ("V4" to "V6"), and a "B2" will be at around 5.13 in difficulty or harder ("V7" and up). Where a Gill rating is provided, it may include a plus to denote problems that fall in the gray area between "B" ratings (e.g., a "B1+" might seem harder than your average "B1" problem but not so difficult that anybody thinks it deserves a "B2" grade). There are a handful of "B1" problems and only a very few established "B2" problems at Schurman Rock, although there are many hard problems just waiting to be imagined.

If you are one of those bouldering purists who believes a Gill "B1" problem has to be as hard as the current hardest free-climbing route, you will be disappointed. The current hardest free climb is rated 5.15d. Nobody climbs that hard; not at Schurman Rock anyway. Local guides to artificial climbing walls have consistently equated "B1" with at least "5.12" and a "B2" with "5.13" and harder. The old theory was that there were no individual moves harder than 5.13, and a 5.14 route consisted a series of 5.13 cruxes that cumulatively added up to 5.14 difficulty rather than having a single 5.14 move. Apparently there are now 5.14 routes that do have an individual move that is considered 5.14, and boulder problems with individual moves that equate to 5.15 on the YDS scale. If you can climb that hard, good for you; there's nothing at Schurman Rock anywhere near that difficulty—at least, not yet.

Of course, this is all very general and, as Beckey suggested, the ratings are subject to a variety of interpretations. One person's

"MODERATE" might be another person's "HARD," just as one person's "V2" might be another person's "V3," and the V Scale has been adjusted downward at some climbing gyms, making an old-school "V3" much harder than a current "V3." Fortunately, Schurman Rock is not a crucible for development of world-class boulderers pushing the limits of the Sherman scale; it's a rock designed for kids to learn to climb on that also happens to have some fun boulder problems that climbers of all ages and abilities can enjoy, some of which are easy, some moderate, some difficult, some hard. The ratings are relative and subjective; what really matters is how easy, hard, or too hard a given boulder problem seems to you.

What's the rating? Who cares if you're having fun.

If none of this makes any sense to you, don't worry; it doesn't make any sense to anybody but those unfortunate climbers who are obsessed with the numerical ranking of their climbing ability. The spirit of bouldering isn't climbing your way up a number scale; it's challenging yourself against a given route or problem to see if you can do it, solving the problem of working out the moves for your own personal enjoyment, whether it's easy, hard, or too hard.

So don't worry about whether a problem is easy, hard, V2, 5.12, or B2; it doesn't matter. Just climb what you can, challenge yourself to achieve in the future what might seem impossible to you now, and above all, have fun!

BOULDERING SAFETY

> Don't be reluctant to put on a rope if you think you may come off from more than a few feet above the ground - thirty or forty years from now your back, knees, ankles, and feet will thank you . . .

> –John Gill

Although bouldering has been called "rock without risk," anybody who has bouldered seriously for any length of time knows that isn't true. You don't have to crater from the crux move of *Midnight Lightning* (a famous hard boulder problem in Yosemite) to end up with a broken wrist; you can do that falling off of Schurman Rock despite the layer of cushioning gravel. If you're climbing off the ground, even a few feet, no matter how difficult the problem or how many pads you use, there's always a possibility you can get hurt when you fall off or have to jump off to bail from a problem that's over your head.

Schurman Rock was designed to provide a safe place to learn and practice climbing, and overall it is a safe place to climb. Still, there are a lot of ways to get hurt while climbing, even at Schurman Rock. If you're bouldering, you're going to fall off; it's a given. Falling or bailing off a given problem from any height could possibly result in a sprained or broken ankle, wrist, knee, elbow; torn cartilage or a ruptured tendon; dislocated shoulder or hip; a strained or broken neck or back; or a concussion or skull fracture, even if you use pads or have a spotter. You could get stung by a bee, wasp, or hornet; bitten by a spider; or attacked by a territorial owl, eagle, or hummingbird. A dog could bite you; a tree limb could fall on you. A kid could hit you in the eye with a rock. You could slip on wet moss or a slug. You never know.

With an alert spotter and a crash pad, bouldering
can be a relatively safe activity.

Climbers have miraculously survived long, unroped falls off of
the highest climbing walls without serious injury; others have not
been so lucky. Falling off isn't even required to suffer a serious injury;
climbers have suffered dislocated or broken fingers, hands, and spiral

fractures, not to mention torn or ruptured tendons and ligaments, among other injuries, without even falling off. But falling or jumping off the rock greatly increases your chances of injury, especially if you hit something or land on somebody on your way down. Even landing wrong on your bouldering pad or getting wrapped up in your toprope can result in injury. So climb carefully!

In bouldering, as in judo and other martial arts, learning how to fall and land properly is important because you will definitely fall off at some point while bouldering. Although falling off is not a desired result in climbing, it is to be expected. "If you aren't falling, you aren't trying," as they say. So, it is important not only to learn good climbing technique, but also proper falling/landing technique and how to spot your fellow boulderers; and if you are using a toprope, knowing some basic rope craft, such as knots and belay technique, is vitally important. (Since this isn't a climbing instruction book, you'll have to learn those on your own.)

Kids who try to climb Schurman Rock and chicken out halfway up usually ask the same question: "How do I get down." As John Sherman, author of *Better Bouldering*, says, the first rule of bouldering is to know how you will get down before you start up. Fortunately, descending from Schurman Rock is easy; just scramble down the "staircase" on the north side and you're down.

Kids tend to get stuck on top of the Needle; since there isn't an easy way off the top, they have to either climb down the way they came up or make the big step across to the main rock; both options are scary and a little dangerous for the uninitiated. Adults don't seem to have as much of a problem with stepping across the gap, but it's still high up with a bad landing and should not be taken lightly. Most kids get across the step-across just fine although a belay from above would be safer; others manage to climb down safely, but may need some assistance or a spot. However, with the first rule of bouldering in mind, you should figure out how you will get down before you get yourself stuck.

"Should I jump down?" is a frequent question asked by kids who get stuck. No, of course not! You should have a strategy for bailing off of a problem if it proves too difficult for you, whether your plan is climbing down, traversing off, or grabbing a nearby jug and finishing up an easier route. Jumping off is a popular exit strategy, especially among kids, but it's a bad habit to get into as can lead to injury either due to a bad landing or the cumulative effect of repeated hard landings. Jumping off is inviting injury; don't do it!

Old-school toproping on Schurman Rock, 1977.
Photo: Camp Long collection.

At Schurman Rock, you can usually bail off by grabbing a big hold and climbing up or down an easier way, but on real boulders you may have to bail dynamically (not jumping so much as letting go in a way that positions you to land as safely as possible), which is where a pad can come in handy, especially if the landing is on broken ground or involves jagged rocks. There is a "safe" way to fall and land in many sports, that generally involves landing on your feet with your legs apart (in "athletic position"), absorbing the energy of the fall with your knees before rolling onto your back with your head tucked to your chest to avoid smacking your skull. You don't want to land stiff-legged or with your feet together like an Olympic gymnast; that's a sure way to get hurt. You also don't want to absorb all of the energy of the fall with your knees, especially a longer fall. It is vitally important that you inspect the landing before you start climbing so you know what to avoid if you fall off; if you have a small landing area, or the landing is bordered by rocks, trees, metal railings, or the like, you don't want to drop and roll because you might hit your head; you may want a spotter, a pad, or even a helmet.

Of course, if you toprope, you don't have to worry so much about a bad landing, as long as you've set up your toprope and tied in correctly and have a reliable belayer. Belay and rappel technique are fairly specialized and must be learned from an experienced instructor. You don't need a lot of fancy gear to toprope safely; you can get by with just a sling, carabiner, and a rope, tying in with a bowline-on-a-coil knot and using a hip belay, if you know what you are doing. You can probably also rappel safely enough without a lot of gear, if you learn and execute the Dulfersitz technique perfectly (the way they taught the kids how to do it back in Clark Schurman's day), although having a harness, belay/rappel device, and locking carabiner make both belaying and rappelling much safer and enjoyable.

Still, this doesn't mean that you won't get hurt if you fall off from any height, even on a toprope People get badly hurt from tripping while walking on a sidewalk after falling from zero feet up, or tripping over their dog. It's easy to hit your elbow, knee, or head on the rock even while toproped. So, whether you climb roped or unroped, with or without a pad, spotter, or helmet, eight inches or eight feet off the ground, be alert, climb carefully, and have a plan.

That said, some problems are more objectively hazardous than others, usually due to height or bad fall potential. Most problems in this guide have fairly clean fall lines onto gravel, but there are some problems that have a boulder or adjacent wall directly below or behind the climber, increasing the likelihood that you might sprain or break something or smack your head hard if you fall off. I will mention objective hazards that I know of, and suggest safety precautions for any particularly hazardous problem. However, climbing is inherently dangerous and I can't foresee or warn of every possible way that users of this guide might injure themselves. Some people have to be told the rock is slippery when wet.

Common sense dictates that if there's a boulder or slab below your feet or a slab, wall, or bench behind your head, or the problem is twenty feet high, it's more likely you could get hurt if you fell off of that problem than a similar problem closer to the ground with a cushy landing and nothing to hit your head on. So, take a look around, avoid any obvious objective hazards, and take appropriate precautions to avoid hurting yourself.

It's a good idea to have a spotter if you're climbing unroped.

Don't hesitate to use a toprope. Your knees will thank you.
Photo: Camp Long collection.

The rock is at most about twenty feet high, and most of the problems end with several large holds or ledges, making falling off from high up fairly unlikely unless you are purposely trying to do hard moves high off the deck or playing around carelessly on the summit. That said, falling off happens, and the rock is high enough off the ground that a fall could result in serious injury or even death. The rock has built-in safety features, including anchor bolts for toproping and belaying, and a loose gravel base to help absorb the impact of a fall, but an awkward or unexpected fall in the wrong place from even a few feet up could result in a bad landing and sprained or broken ankle, knee, or wrist, or a head, neck, or spinal injury.

A good toproping setup, with a long sling tied to an anchor running over the edge to eliminate rope drag. Photo courtesy Mountain Madness.

A majority of Schurman Rock climbers climb unroped, scrambling or bouldering up or around the rock, and even fall off sometimes without getting seriously hurt, but beginning or inexperienced climbers should be roped up and belayed unless bouldering close to the ground, and in that case, they should have a spotter at a minimum. For safety and liability reasons, all climbing courses on the rock require that climbers tie in and wear helmets. Outside of the requirements of an organized class, the decision to rope up or wear a helmet is up to each individual climber. I recommend that children wear a helmet whenever climbing on or around the rock; although not rated for climbing, a bike or skate helmet is better than no helmet.

As John Gill, who is regarded as the godfather of American bouldering, wisely advises, if there's a chance you are going to fall off from even a few feet above the ground, you should use a toprope to spare yourself not only the risk of imminent injury, but also the cumulative effect of repeated hard landings that will take a toll on your back, knees, ankles, and feet. Ring anchors are installed on all sides of the rock to facilitate toproping and rappelling. If you toprope, please sling the anchors instead of running your rope through the rings, to avoid unnecessary wear. Also, it is wise to equalize two anchors for toproping, since these are old iron ring bolts set in concrete, seemingly solid but you never know.

A bad toproping setup. Don't run the rope directly
through the bolts or over the edges!

Loose gravel has been added around the base of the rock, which offers some shock absorption for falling climbers, but not much, especially given the gravel's tendency to creep downhill, away from the base of the rock, and the fact that kids regularly pick up handfuls of the stuff and throw it in the bushes or at each other, leaving a sometimes-thin layer close to the base of the rock that provides illusory protection at best. Don't expect the gravel to cushion a fall like at the U.W. Rock or like the shredded-tire base at the

Mountaineers' climbing wall; it won't. It won't be anything like the cushy mats at the climbing gym, either. The impact can be like landing on a concrete sidewalk in places, making use of a bouldering pad or toprope a good idea if you are climbing high off the ground on thin holds.

Because Schurman Rock is eighty years old and rocks do occasionally come loose or fall out, climbers should take care to avoid dislodging them. As in the mountains, it is a good idea to test holds before using them, especially holds at the tops of the walls, which are more prone to pulling out due to the horizontal forces imposed by climbers yanking on them when topping out on a given wall. Indeed, several rocks along the top row have come out over the years, leaving gaps like missing teeth. As in the mountains, test suspect holds by hitting them gently with the side of your hand or fist once or twice before committing to them (you'll hear a hollow thud when you hit a couple of them—use those holds carefully or avoid them), and try to exert force in the direction least likely to shear off a given hold even if it doesn't seem loose. It is generally no more difficult to top out without pulling outward on the top holds; in most cases, you can use the concrete in the gaps between holds just as well, but check the concrete, too, as it can be flaky in places and could break off.

After eight decades of use by thousands of climbers, some of the holds on Schurman Rock have become quite polished and slick. You will think you are securely attached to a big hold and then – woosh! – come slipping right off of it unexpectedly. The slickest holds are polished to a high shine and actually reflect sunlight; others are more insidious, lurking here and there on the rock waiting for some unsuspecting climber to grab or step on them. The holds seem slickest on hot summer days, when even sticky-soled climbing shoes have a hard time staying stuck. And, yes, the rock is slippery when wet! If you're climbing when it's raining or just after, the holds are slippery. Climb carefully and test holds before committing to them so you don't come sailing off.

Although the rock was designed to be climbed by kids, they may pose the greatest hazard for themselves and other climbers. Kids are drawn to the rock and love to play all over and around it which, unfortunately, means they are often running around directly under a climber, oblivious to the danger of being landed on or having climbing gear dropped on them. (Same with dogs, which are supposed to be on leash but are often running around loose, annoying everybody except their oblivious owners.) Despite their daring exploits on the rock and admonitions from their parents to get down before they hurt themselves, kids seem to manage to get up and down the rock quite frequently without hurting themselves too badly, although I am expecting a child to fall off the top someday given the shenanigans that go on up there when kids are playing unsupervised on the rock. If you're running up and around the rock, chasing your friends, and throwing gravel at each other, you're more likely to trip, slip, fall, and get hurt.

Kids who approach climbing more seriously tend to not get hurt; they seem to have the sense to avoid dangerous situations and climb down when the going gets scary. Others seem to climb up oblivious to the danger, then get stuck ten feet off the ground, unable to move up or down, begging to be rescued, sometimes jumping down—a sure way to get hurt. And then there are those who wander around the base of the rock, oblivious to the danger of others climbing above them. Children should be supervised, kept out from under other climbers, and, when appropriate, belayed or at least spotted by an adult. Kids climbing on the rock or playing around below it while others are climbing should ideally be wearing a helmet. Nobody wants a kid to fall off the rock and get hurt; thankfully, thousands of kids seem to get up and down the rock ever year without incident. Let's keep it that way!

But, again, this is not a climbing instruction book. I urge you to learn climbing and safety techniques from a qualified instructor or guide. Until then, don't climb any higher than you are willing to fall. Most climbing gyms disallow unroped climbing higher than 10 or 12 feet above the mats, a height that has been deemed "safe" for bouldering in those particular gyms; Schurman Rock is about 20 feet high in some places and doesn't have thick, cushy landing mats, so do the math. On most of the walls, the "hard" climbing ends on a ledge that is 9 to 11 feet up, from where you can "walk" off via a foot traverse or do a hand traverse to an easy finish or downclimb, and you have a gravel landing, such as it is; so for the most part bouldering at Schurman Rock is relatively safe except on the upper sections of a few of the walls and any time you are climbing above a ledge or protruding rock or boulder.

A group of kids waits their turn to climb Schurman Rock.
Photo courtesy Mountain Madness.

Finally, beware of spiders living in the cracks and gaps in the rock here and there (they bite), hornets hunting the spiders (they sting), slugs (they slime up the holds), and mosquitoes which come out in droves on humid spring and summer evenings (annoying!). Occasionally, someone lets their dog run amok on and around the rock which, aside from being really annoying, can present a safety hazard, especially if the dog is aggressive, provoking other dogs, or sniffing or pawing at everybody. Please keep your dog leashed and tied up away from the rock to avoid creating a hazard.

For a good discussion of bouldering technique and safety, refer to John Sherman's *Better Bouldering* (Falcon 2012).

ROUTES AND BOULDER PROBLEMS

> It's not as easy as it might look, despite the lack of altitude. One adult group, attempting advanced work, sent member after member to try a "traverse" across a smooth slab, with feet only a yard or so from the ground. The surface to be crossed was only six feet wide... But nobody made it until two and a half hours.
>
> "Man-Made Peak Challenges
> Hardiest of Mountaineers"
> *The Seattle Star*, February 19, 1947

Okay, now to the fun stuff! As Clark Schurman's 1938 *Mountaineer* article and the 1947 *Seattle Star* article quoted above attest, climbers have been working out distinct routes and boulder problems on Schurman Rock since it was first built. The following is a selection of some of the dozens of "routes" or boulder problems at Schurman Rock, including several of Clark Schurman's original "short bits." The problems are described in a counter-clockwise direction starting from the left edge of the West Face, with problems on the Needle described last.

This selection is by no means exhaustive; I have selected some of the more obvious "natural" lines since those are what a majority of climbers start with, and added some of the better contrived problems, but not all of them. There are well over a hundred established problems on the rock, and many more possible problems to be contrived, so don't let this guide limit your exploration of Schurman Rock; by all means, make up your own problems and call them whatever you like. Just don't be sure Fred Beckey didn't climb them first.

One might think a guide to routes on an artificial climbing wall is a silly thing. Clark Schurman didn't think so. His 1938 *Mountaineer* article included a rough guide to twenty-two different problems ("short bits" he called them), including illustrations of four of the problems. You can still climb most of Schurman's original routes, and several of them are included in this guide for historical reference.

Some of them, such as the overhang problems and "Cooning place via broad chimney," no longer exist due to modification of the rock (addition of a buttress on the southeast side that blocked the Prusik overhang and chimney). A couple of them, such as "Needle by lariat" or "Chockstone treated as impassable without rope" could still be done using a rope, one supposes, although modern climbers usually find more sport in ascending the walls without rope tricks. Who knows, though; it might be fun to bring a rope and lasso the Needle!

Use the "north ramp" or "stairway" to set up a toprope or descend if it isn't crowded with kids, or downclimb an easy problem on any side of the rock. Above all, climb safely, and have fun!

NORTH SIDE

The north side of the rock is a low-angle, blocky slope that is regularly climbed by dozens of kids nearly every day. Clark Schurman mentioned two of the north side routes in his 1938 article. "The Staircase" may be the most-climbed route in the world, ever.

"The Staircase" (1), "North Ramp" (2), and "À Cheval" (3).

1. "THE STAIRCASE" (Easy) – The standard route to the top, up the big boulders and ledges on the north side. An easy scramble for almost everybody except babies, it has probably been climbed more than a million times since 1939. It's slick in a couple of places, so watch your step, especially on the way down. If you want to make this more challenging, try hopping up it on one foot, climbing it upside-down, or juggling as you ascend.

2. "NORTH RAMP" (Easy) – A short slabby wall just right of the easy route that is a little more challenging than the big ledges. It's also a fun little no-hands problem.

WEST FACE

The west side of Schurman Rock is a long, flat, almost vertical wall. There are many possible problems here, especially if you follow Clark Schurman's lead and ignore the "gift-rocks" and use only "wrinkles" and "discolorations" to ascend or traverse. The left side of the wall has a ledge about ten feet up, making it a good bouldering wall; you can climb up to the ledge then hand traverse a few moves to the left and finish up easy terrain or down the crack to descend. The right side of the wall has an iron bolt that can be used to practice lead climbing, either as a protection point or as an anchor to practice leapfrogging (changing leaders on a multi-pitch route); it's a beefy bolt that seems pretty solid for having been in place for eighty years but you never know. Likewise, the rocks along the top of the crenellated wall seem pretty solid, but a few have come loose over the years, so go easy on them when topping out. The harder you pull on a single rock while topping out, the more likely it will pull off and land on your face when you hit the ground. You can top out just as easily without yanking hard on the rocks. The problems are listed from left to right.

3. "À CHEVAL" (Easy) – This is the rounded, low-angle arête on the far-left edge of the West Face, a feature specifically designed by Clark Schurman to allow climbers to learn the *à cheval* technique (like riding a horse), putting their "fifth point of suspension" to use because "it's important to know how to sit and edge along." Despite Schurman's good intentions, the problem is more easily and naturally

climbed standing up using friction and balance; it's more secure that way if you are barefoot or are wearing rock shoes, but kind of slick in tennis shoes; if your feet slip, there's little to hold onto so you'd fall right off. This is a challenging no-hands problem; it's also kind of dangerous since a slip at the wrong place could result in a bad fall.

West Face routes, "Arachnid Crack" Area.

4. "ARACHNID CRACK" (EASY) – This is the only "crack" on the west side of the rock. It is one of the "short bits" identified in Clark Schurman's 1938 article, and is still regularly ascended by adventuresome children if adults aren't there to discourage them. Easiest if you layback up the right edge of the crack; a little more challenging if you do it as a layback up the left edge. You can also climb it with hand stacks, knee-bars, or by Gastoning if you're into that sort of thing. There are usually several spiders living in the back of the crack, so don't stick your hands in there too far.

5. "WEST FACE" (Easy) – Climb the steep wall to the right of the crack using any or all of the available holds. There are a dozen or more possible variations, climbing straight up here or there, using only this or that rock, using only one hand or only index fingers, or eliminating some or all of the various "gift-holds" including the ledge, using only the "wrinkles" and "discolorations," or any combination of the above. One can boulder up to the ledge then exit to the left and finish up the final crack moves or downclimb the crack to escape if the headwall proves too daunting.

6. "TOY BLOCKS" (Moderate) – One of the many possible variations on the West Face, eliminating all but four large rocks for hands and feet. It is an "English" problem that is easiest if you allow features for the feet in addition to the assigned rocks; more difficult as a pure English problem limited to only the four rocks as hand- and footholds. Manteling onto the highest rock may be the crux.

7. "THE EGG" (Moderate) – Climb directly up to the white, egg-shaped rock set Humpty Dumpty-like at the top of the middle section of the West Face, using any holds including the intermediate ledges for hands and feet. Once you're standing on the ledge, you can traverse off to the left if the final moves up the headwall seem too high off the ground.

8. "HUMPTY DANCE I" and "HUMPTY DANCE II" (Difficult) – Two four-rock problems following the line of "The Egg" without using any of the intermediate ledge holds, instead reaching past and then high-stepping from the big gray block to one of the holds above the ledges or the other. One version uses the lowest (smaller left) hold above the ledges and skips the next good (larger right) hold; the other version does the opposite. The four rocks and concrete features are all you are allowed for the hands; any holds except the ledges are allowed for the feet, except the one rock that must be eliminated entirely on each problem. Landing on the ledge from the final moves would make for a "great fall."

9. "THE BULGE" (Moderate) – Ascend directly up to and over the "bulge," a protruding granite boulder above the ledge. Easier if you climb a little to the left or right of the bulge instead of climbing

directly past it. There are several eliminate variations, such as not using the ledge, or allowing only four rocks, and so on.

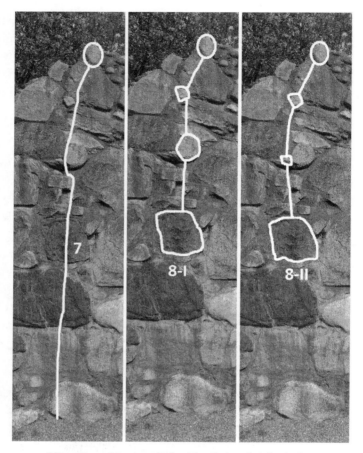

West Face Routes, "The Egg" detail. The ledge
holds are off limits for the "Humpty Dance" problems.

10. "SHOULDER STAND" (MODERATE) – Clark Schurman described a route involving a shoulder stand to reach a ledge, followed by an eleven-foot finger traverse or a foot traverse around the "bulge." This is it. You can dispense with the shoulder stand and just free-climb up to the ledge using the pedestal, which appears to have been added on later so you can do the shoulder-stand move without having to actually stand on a Boy Scout. You can eliminate the pedestal and just climb the wall without it. However you do it, traverse leftward along the ledge past the bulge and up.

West Face routes, "The Bulge" area.

11. "OZONE HOLE" (MODERATE) – Climb up to and past the rectangular "hole" on the right side of the West Face, staying left of the ring bolt. To make it more interesting, don't use the pedestal or the ledge. As with other problems above ledges, there is bad fall potential as hitting the ledge could knock you off balance and land you on your head.

12. "WEST COLUMN" (MODERATE) – Climb the buttress on the left side of "CHOCKSTONE CHIMNEY" using any holds on the buttress and its arête, staying right of the ring bolt to make it more direct. Easier if you use all available holds including the big ledge, but

more sporting if you stick to holds on the column face proper. It is probably wise not to pull too hard on the exit hold; it seems solid now, but also seems to be a prime candidate to lever off someday if somebody wrenches on it too hard the wrong way.

13. "CHOCKSTONE CHIMNEY" (EASY) – The big chimney with the "chockstone" halfway up. The chimney is 30 inches wide according to Clark Schurman, and with the chockstone in the way, is more amenable to stemming than classic feet-and-back chimney technique. The chimney is easiest if you use the chockstone, especially to stand on (all the kids do); more difficult if you don't use it. In his 1938 guide, Schurman mentioned two ways of climbing this chimney: "without help" of the chockstone and "impassable without rope." Since chockstones on real rock climbs tend to be loose and unstable, you should do it without using the chockstone as Schurman intended. A fall onto the chockstone would probably hurt, so climb carefully above it especially if you are unroped.

14. "SOUTH COLUMN" (DIFFICULT) – The distinct pillar on the right side of "CHOCKSTONE CHIMNEY," one of the hardest and steepest natural lines on the rock. There really aren't any "gift-holds" on this one; it is a difficult problem even if you allow use of every hold on and around each arête; quite hard if you climb the "SOUTH COLUMN DIRECT" variation using only holds on the face of the column proper and eliminating all of the holds on or around either arête. The hardest moves are at the top; landing on the boulder at the base would probably be painful; toprope, pad, or spotter recommended, especially if you are doing the harder variation.

15. "NEEDLE CHIMNEY" (EASY OR MODERATE) – The narrow chimney between the main wall and the detached tower; at 25 inches in width, this chimney is a little more cramped than the other, providing more realistic knee-and-back chimney practice. More difficult with your back on the main wall. You can make it more difficult by relying solely on your exemplary chimneying skills using only the smooth chimney face instead of positive holds. You can also face climb up either wall of the chimney; the tower side is thin and kind of hard. The landing is a solid granite boulder, so climb carefully if unroped.

West Face routes, "Chockstone Chimney" area.

16. "WEST FACE TRAVERSE" (Easy to B2) – Traverse across the West Face in either direction. Easiest if you hand or foot traverse the big ledge; more difficult if you stay below the ledge. The lower you traverse on the wall, the more difficult it is. Once you've mastered the traverse in one direction, work it the other way, then start eliminating holds, using smaller and smaller holds, concrete holds, underclings or side-pulls only, limiting the number of rocks you use for the hands, using only holds below eye level, eliminating all of the "good" footholds, traversing one-handed, and so on. Make up any traverse you like, as hard as you like; there are dozens of possible variations.

17. "TWO-ROCK TRAVERSE" (HARD) – One of the West Face traverse variations, using only two concrete holds and two rocks for hands, any rocks for the feet but don't use the pedestal on the right if you can avoid it (you can), if only to make it more fun. You can't say you've done it until you've done it both ways. There are several other two-, three-, four-, and five-rock traverses, and one that uses concrete holds only all the way across. Make up a "new" one. Have fun!

SOUTH FACE

The South Face is a steep wall, vertical to overhanging in places, intersected by various ledges. It has several enjoyable problems, some of the best on the rock. This wall warms up nicely on sunny winter days, and due to sun exposure is usually the first wall to dry off after it stops raining. Fred Beckey is pictured climbing this wall in *Climbing in North America*, making it quite the sought-after climb. Most of the problems have a clean landing on flat, thin gravel, but a few have potentially bad landings, so use a pad, spotter, or toprope wherever the landing seems sketchy.

18. "THE STEPS" (EASY) – Use any holds you like to get up to the "steps," a series of big holds and ledges near the top of the wall on the left side. Clark Schurman designed the steps to provide a "gradual start" for rappelling practice down this side of the rock; that may be, but they make nice, big hand- and footholds, making this route popular with the kids. You can start on the big boulder at the base of the chimney, or start from the ground to add an extra move. It is

easier the farther left you climb since that's where the bigger holds are. Several variations are possible, so if it seems too easy for you, eliminate some holds. Potential bad landing on the boulder if you're climbing up the left side.

Some routes up the South Face. Make up your own!

19. "LINE OF FLIGHT" (DIFFICULT) – A variations of "THE STEPS," a reachy problem climbing the wall using only three rocks for the hands to reach the top; all rocks allowed for the feet. Easier if you are taller or have a long reach. If you can't make the reach to the third rock, you could try a dyno, use a lower third rock, or try an entirely different combination of three rocks.

"Line of Flight" (19), "Crimp Fest" (25), and "Razor's Edge" (32).

20. "THE PROW" (MODERATE) – Climb straight up the steepest part of the wall to the prow/arête in the middle of the South Face, then up the rocks forming the prow to the top. You don't have to limit yourself to only the rocks on the prow as you ascend, but it's not all that difficult to climb the prow directly once you reach it, and almost feels exposed near the top.

21. "TYROMANIA" (DIFFICULT) – A reachy, juggy line up the prow using only four rocks for the hands; all rocks allowed for the feet.

You can use any part of the four rocks as a handhold, but don't use the little embedded rock above the second rock; it's a great hold, but it's a separate rock that is out of bounds for this problem.

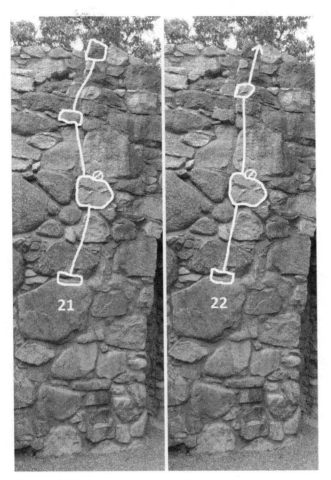

"Tyromania" (21) and "Empty Hand" (22).

22. "EMPTY HAND" (HARD) – A three-rock problem up the prow, this one involving two powerful lunges in a row, first from the large gray rock to the higher granite block (using any part of that block but not the separate smaller rocks just above it), then all the way to the upper ledge before a much easier final move to the "summit." The second lunge is kind of up there and committing; a pad or spotter (or both) is recommended. Any part of the designated rocks is allowed for the hands; any holds allowed for the feet.

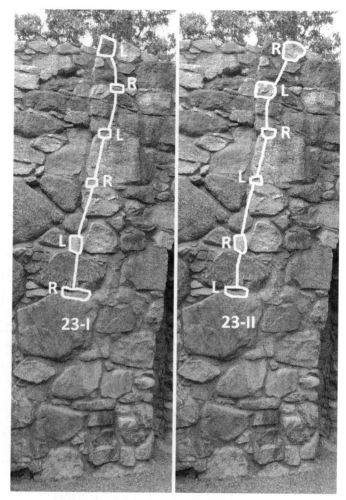

"Synchronicity I" and "Synchronicity II."

23. "SYNCHRONICITY I" and "SYNCHRONICITY II" (DIFFICULT) – Two "synchronized" problems starting from the horizontal hold on top of the large gray boulder and climbing a series of rocks up the prow to the top for the hands; all rocks allowed for the feet. One version starts with the right hand, the other with the left; each version finishes on a different rock to top out, although just grabbing the top wherever is fine. For that matter, you don't have to synchronize the moves; it's a fun problem any way you do it.

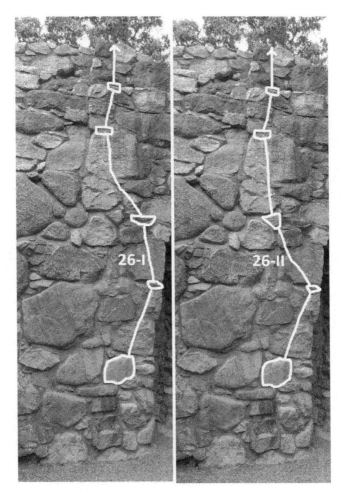

"Old Man's Folly" variations.

24. "SALATHÉ WALL" (MODERATE) – Given its position in relation to "The Nose" of Schurman Rock, this steepest portion of the South Face is reminiscent of the *Salathé Wall* route on El Capitan in Yosemite, only easier and not quite as imposing. Climb directly up the South Face staying between the prow on the left and the arête on the right and not using either of them, only holds on the face itself. Use any combination of holds you like; once you've done it one way, try it another, or eliminate some holds; several variations are possible, some of which are quite difficult. If you want to get carried away, climb it 167 times in a row (or 84 times to the top and down) which would equal about 3,000 feet of vertical climbing, an "El Cap day."

"Anderson Memorial" (29) and "Razor's Edge" (32).

25. "CRIMP FEST" (HARD) – One of the possible variations of the South Face, a sit-down start problem linking several of the crimpiest edges on the wall. Only the six holds shown are allowed for the hands to reach the top; use any rocks for the feet. Can be done without the sit-down start, using the second hold as the opening hold instead. Once you've done it, try eliminating one of the holds to make it ridiculously hard.

26. "OLD MAN'S FOLLY" (HARD) – More sit-down start variations, one linking the pinch hold on the right with the flake, the other using the hold just left of the flake; use any rocks for the feet. One variation is definitely more difficult than the other. The crux move can be done as a static or dynamic move. The sit-down start is not required; use the pinch hold as the opening hold if you prefer.

27. "FLY OR DIE" (HARD) – A double-lunge problem, this one striking rightward from the gray block to the flake to the protruding rock (the "prow" or "beak") at the top of the alcove, then to the ledge and the top; use any rocks for the feet. The lunge to the beak is a little off the deck with bad landing potential, so don't blow it. Can be done without lunging, but seems more difficult that way. Easier and less committing if you use an intermediate handhold instead of lunging all the way from the flake to the beak. If you blow the lunge, you could land badly against the opposite wall of the alcove. Add a sit-down start to make it harder.

28. "ARÊTE DIRECT" (HARD) – Climb the arête on the right side of the South Face using only rocks on the arête itself for the hands and feet, with no stemming or scumming out on the buttress wall across the alcove. Because your feet stay to the right but your upper body is forced left, the final move is a long, off-balance reach from the "beak" to the ledge; it's kind of dicey, with bad landing potential if you blow it, so take appropriate precautions. Can be done using only three rocks for hands to the ledge, which makes it much harder.

29. "LLOYD & MARY ANDERSON MEMORIAL ROUTE" (MODERATE) – A fun problem honoring the memory of Lloyd and Mary Anderson, important figures in the Seattle climbing scene back when Schurman Rock was constructed and long after. This problem links the arête on the right with the prow on the left; start up the arête then traverse face holds leftward across the wall to the prow, then layback and palm up the prow to the top. You can make this more difficult by eliminating all but one or two of the face holds on the traverse.

30. "THE ALCOVE" (MODERATE) – Climb up the half-chimney between the South Face and Southwest Buttress however you like;

"Fly or Die" (27) and sit-down start
variation, and the classic "Beckey Route" (33).

the chimney ends ten feet up, forcing you to face climb the slightly
overhanging headwall to the top. There are several ways to climb the
chimney. You can use proper chimney technique for a couple of
moves; stem up the opposing walls which is kind of fun; or face
climb using the big holds in the back of the alcove which is kind of
scary because of all the spiders living in there. A fairly hard variation
goes from the rectangular block in the back of the alcove all the way
to the "beak," a long reach or dynamic move with bad fall potential,
best reserved for your better judgment.

SOUTHEAST BUTTRESS ("THE NOSE")

There is a photo in *Challenge of the North Cascades* of Fred Beckey "exercising" on Schurman Rock. In the photo, Beckey is seen stemming facing out across a wide corner or chimney. This is the "broad chimney" mentioned in Clark Schurman's 1938 article. For some reason, most probably to shore up the overhanging wall to prevent it from collapsing, a buttress was added to the rock within a couple of years of the rock's completion. In addition to the chimney, one imagines there used to be one or two difficult routes up the overhanging wall that, alas, have been walled in by the buttress. The closest you can come to experiencing the overhanging wall in its original state is to climb the "Arête Direct" problem. The buttress has many of the easiest problems on Schurman Rock owing to its relatively low angle and abundance of good-size holds, and is regularly ascended by unsupervised children. You can make up any number of problems here by eliminating "gift-holds" and so on, including several one- and two-handed problems and even a no-hands problem.

31. "THE NOSE" (Easy) – The Southeast Buttress of Schurman Rock forms a distinct prow reminiscent of the Nose of El Capitan, only smaller and not as difficult to climb. It is, in fact, one of the easier routes up the rock, although it is still a challenge to the many kids who try it daily. Climb the buttress any way you like. There are dozens of possible problems using any combination of holds—four rocks, three rocks, two rocks, synchronized, "English," and so on. The fewer or smaller holds you use, the more difficult it becomes. If it seems too easy for you one way, try it another way, then try it one handed, with index fingers or pinkies only, or "ham-handed" (with closed fists). It can even be climbed with no hands, an ultimate test of balance; good luck with that one! If you climb it 167 times in a row (or all the way up and down 84 times), you would have climbed 3,000 vertical feet, the same distance as the real *Nose* route; have fun with that! Time yourself; you might just beat the record.

32. "RAZOR'S EDGE" (Difficult) – This problem climbs the left side of the Nose buttress using six rocks for the hands to get to the top; use any rocks for the feet. There's a sharp horizontal edge

Southeast Buttress (left) and East Face (right).

halfway up that's thin but solid; the final hold is even thinner and the final move is committing and kind of difficult; bad fall potential if you blow the last move. Several variations and eliminations are possible; it can be done using as few as three rocks for the hands, or as an "English" problem. It has even been done using only the index fingers of either hand; don't get carried away by trying it pinkies-only, though; that would be silly.

More Routes on The Nose and East Face.

33. "THE BECKEY ROUTE" (Easy) – The late Fred Beckey is pictured on this problem in *Climbing in North America*, making it the

most iconic route at Schurman Rock. Climb the buttress, traverse obliquely leftward from ledge to ledge, and finish up the prow, using whatever holds you like.

EAST FACE

The eastern face of Schurman Rock is a flat wall with a narrow ledge above it, capped by a short overhanging wall. The lower half of the wall is a good bouldering wall for beginners since it's only ten feet high to the ledge, which offers an easy exit. The ledge (what Clark Schurman called the "cooning ledge," describing the technique of climbing along on all fours) kind of ruins the effect of climbing out the overhang, especially for tall climbers who can easily reach from the ledge to the jugs and miss the fun of the overhang entirely.

34. "WALL OF THE EARLY MORNING LIGHT" ("DAWN WALL") (MODERATE) – Climb the steep wall just right of the Nose, which is reminiscent of the *Dawn Wall* on El Capitan, not so much because it has multiple pitches of finger-ripping 5.14 moves, but rather because it sublimely captures the early morning light during the summer months. Moderately difficult if you climb as straight up as possible up to and through the slightly overhanging finish without using the ledges or big holds on either side. You can eliminate holds to make this problem more difficult. Once you've done it the "easy" way, try it without any of the "good" holds.

35. "BATSO'S REVENGE" (HARD) – An athletic problem ascending the "DAWN WALL" using only the two rocks shown for the hands to the top; all rocks allowed for the feet but not the ledges on either side. Odds are you can't reach the first rock from the ground even if you are tall and have a long reach; keep trying, you'll figure it out, just like those climbers who don't have a long reach have to figure out how to do all those long-reach problems.

36. "MIKE'S PROBLEM" (HARD) – An "English" problem using only the four rocks shown for hands and feet to the top; no other rocks allowed until the top edge is reached. In fact, no holds other than the four rocks are allowed; that means no concrete features for hands or feet, either.

37. "EAST FACE" (Easy) – The East Face is intersected by a ledge, above which the wall rears to slightly overhanging for a few feet; this is optimistically referred to as the "roof" as it is the most overhanging feature on the rock. Climb up to and over the "roof" whichever way you choose. Schurman suggested there were "three good routes" on the wall, which is true, but more variations can be made up, all of which are made a little more difficult if you don't grab or stand on the ledge but step across it from holds on the lower wall. Some climbers don't top out, but pulling over the roof is the hardest and most enjoyable move on the wall. Test the exit holds before cranking on them, though; they seem solid now but could come loose if you crank too hard.

The infamous "Dime Edge Traverse."

38. "DIME-EDGE TRAVERSE" (B1) – Speaking of eliminating holds, this crimpy traverse crosses the East Face without any handholds except a series of thin "features" occurring "naturally" on the faces of the rocks; you don't get to use the tops, sides, or bottoms of the rocks or any concrete holds for the hands, only the thin edges, flakes, and slopers on the faces of the rocks themselves. Sure, it's super contrived, but once you understand the rules, it's a fun and

challenging traverse that continues across the Nose and South Face all the way to the chimney and beyond. There's an "easy" way to do this problem and a "hard" way; once you've worked it out one way, start eliminating holds. Anything goes for the feet, although there isn't all that much there for the feet in places, either. If you manage it in one direction, try it the other way, or all the way around.

LOWER EAST FACE BOULDER PROBLEMS

The lower half of the East Face is a fun bouldering wall. It is only about ten feet high, with a flat landing and a couple of easy ways down or off, making it perfect for beginning climbers to try bouldering. It also has several one- and two-move problems and traverses that will engage even more experienced boulderers. Any number of contrived problems could be made up here, using this rock or that wrinkle. A dozen of these are described below, but not illustrated so you can have some adventure trying to figure them out. No ratings either; try them, then make up your own!

The Lower East Face is a fun bouldering wall.

"TWO-ROCK PROBLEMS" – Use your choice of any two rocks to reach the ledge; your choice of footholds. The thinner or farther apart the rocks, the more difficult the problem.

"ONE-ROCK PROBLEMS" – Use any single rock you choose to reach the ledge; your choice of footholds. The thinner or lower the rock you use, the more difficult the problem.

"CONCRETE FEATURES ONLY" – Climb the wall using only concrete features for the hands, any rocks for the feet. To make this more difficult, use only one concrete feature, eliminating all others.

"ROCK FEATURES ONLY" – Climb the wall using only rock features for the hands; tops, sides, and bottoms of rocks are not allowed, only the "natural" features on the faces of the rocks; use any rocks for the feet.

"FLAKE LUNGE" – Using only the white granite flake low on the left side of the wall for your hands, lunge all the way to the ledge.

"TWO-HAND LUNGE" – Grab a big rock with both hands and lunge from it to the ledge with both hands at the same time; use any rocks for the feet. You can do it with one hand or the other, but lunging with both hands is more fun.

"FINGER POCKET" – Climb using only the "finger pocket" as a handhold for either or both hands; any rocks for the feet.

"THE CRACK" – Climb the wide crack on the right side of the wall. You can face climb up the rocks, layback up either side, or Gaston; a hand-stack or knee-bar might even work, and there is even rumored to be an actual hand jam. Watch for spiders!

"UNDERCLING PROBLEMS" – Climb or traverse the wall using only undercling holds (or only sidepulls); use any rocks for the feet, or don't use any of them, however you can work it out.

"NO HANDS TO THE LEDGE" – Climb up the wall without using your hands until you can grab the ledge. Running start not required.

"NO HANDS" – Starting on the flat rock at the base of the wall on the right side, climb up to a standing position on the ledge without using your hands.

"TRAVERSE PROBLEMS" – Traverse the wall low or high, in either direction, using whichever holds you like. You can make this harder by eliminating holds, using the finger pocket and concrete holds only, underclings only, one-handed, or whatever.

39. "THE INCREDIBLE JOURNEY" (Hard) – Another eliminate traverse, this one using the fewest number of rocks for the hands as you can to get across the East Face, around the Nose, across the South Face into the chimney, and across the West Face if you get that far. Using just six rocks for the hands all the way around the rock seems to be a fairly hard traverse. Your choice of rocks or concrete features for the hands; use any rocks for the feet.

THE NEEDLE

The Needle is the fifteen-foot-high block detached from the main wall, an easy climb from the south and east sides, much more challenging via its "blank" west face. Clark Schurman called it the "Needle" although it isn't all that sharp and pointy as one would expect a needle to be; it is more often referred to as the "Tower" or "Pinnacle." Whatever you call it, most of Schurman Rock's hardest boulder problems are found on its west face, a flat, vertical wall with a few thin holds and some "wrinkles" and "discolorations" thrown in for fun. Several contrived problems have been made up on this block; the more holds you eliminate, the harder the given problem. There are two ring bolts on the right side of the steep face, which aren't mentioned in Schurman's 1938 article. It seems reasonable to assume they were used to teach and practice rope technique for lead climbing, which would make this an early sport route. Either that, or they were used for direct-aid climbing practice, which is equally likely. In any case, they've been there for some eighty years now, and probably should be treated as historical artifacts and not used for climbing.

The gravel at the base of the bouldering wall (and elsewhere around the rock) is kind of thin in places and the climbing hard enough that you may fall off a few times while working out the moves, so you may want a pad here; your knees will thank you.

The Needle.

"Left Eliminate" (43) and "Rings of Power" (44).

40. "NEEDLE BY LARIAT" (HARD or B1) – Clark Schurman's 1938 article mentions a route called "Needle by lariat"; one supposes this involved lassoing the top of the tower and prusiking up the steep face to the top. Fred Beckey used this technique to make the first ascent of Prusik Peak in 1948; perhaps he learned it here. This problem has gone free, but if you want to get a flavor of some old-

school Schurman Rock climbing, bring a rope and give it a whirl. Most climbers do the free version, or try to; it's an old-school "B1" problem that is usually referred to as *the* boulder problem even though it is only one of many problems on this wall, climbing thin holds up the vertical face, one of those test pieces that separates the "valley sheep" from the "mountain goats" as Schurman used to say. You can climb up the right side, closer to the rings, or more to the left side, using any holds on the face that work for you; the arêtes are out of bounds. The "good" concrete finger pocket on the right at the start was formed fairly recently when some concrete chipped off leaving a convenient edge that makes the first move much easier; the "old-school" version of the problem pretends this new hold isn't there, which makes it more like an actual B1 problem, especially if you climb it in tennis shoes like Fred Beckey used to do.

41. "LEFT ARÊTE PROBLEM" (B1) – Climb the left side of the tower face using the arête edge for your left hand and face holds for your right; the problem isn't really any more difficult if you use only the arête for your left hand, but it is more aesthetic that way and thus more fun. To make it harder, eliminate some holds on the arête or face, or climb the arête directly without using face holds on either wall for the hands, only rocks that form the arête itself for the hands; use any holds for the feet on either side of the arête. This problem has a potentially bad landing on the granite boulder at the base of the chimney, so climb carefully.

42. "RIGHT ARÊTE PROBLEM" (DIFFICULT) – Climb the right side of the tower face using the right edge for your right hand and holds on the face for your left hand, keeping your feet on the face proper all the way to the top. This is a sort of an arête problem except the right edge has some big jugs that make it easier than the left arête, although it is still difficult if you don't use the edge holds for your left hand or feet. You could seemingly climb this problem like a sport route, clipping the ring bolts as you ascend, but the bolts are old and of dubious reliability, historical artifacts really that should probably not be used for anything.

43. "LEFT ELIMINATE" (B1+) – Climb the left side of the tower face using only three rocks for the hands not including any rocks on

the arête; all rocks allowed for the feet. This problem has been done with two combinations of three rocks; either way you do it, it's hard, especially given the poor footholds on this side of the wall. Concrete features are allowed for the hands, except the "big" concrete pocket on the right which, as discussed previously, is a "cheater" hold that makes this and other old-school problems "too easy."

"Lord of the Rings" (45) and "Around the Needle" (47).

44. "RINGS OF POWER" (B1+) – Climb the right side of the tower face using only three rocks for the hands; all rocks allowed for the feet. On this problem, the "new" concrete finger pocket just above the initial rock is not allowed, but other concrete features are permitted for hands or feet. If you use the concrete edge instead of the initial rock, it is a two-rock problem which is still hard, but not quite as hard as the three-rock version since the concrete edge is better positioned and makes the first move much easier.

45. "LORD OF THE RINGS" (B2) – Climb the tower face directly using any rocks for the hands but only features for the feet. To maintain the integrity and difficulty of the original problem, use rocks only for the hands, concrete only for the feet; the "new" concrete hold on the right at the start is off limits as a handhold and can be eliminated as a foothold, although it is still a very hard problem even if you use it. Of course, both arêtes are out of bounds.

46. "INSIDE PASSAGE" (Hard) – Climb the inside wall of the chimney on the Needle side, a steep face climb with a sparse selection of thin holds. It isn't as difficult if you allow use of holds on either arête, or climb it more bear-hug style. The final moves are the hardest, and it has bad landing potential on the granite block and the back wall of the chimney; if you fell off, you could potentially crack your skull and break your ankles both at the same time.

47. "AROUND THE NEEDLE" (Hard) – Traverse all the way around the base of the Needle. You can use all of the "safety steps" if you want to, including the granite boulder at the base of the chimney. It's difficult crossing the west face slab, but there's only one hard move. The real challenge is to traverse around the tower without using any of the ledges or the boulder for your feet.

48. "SAFETY STEPS" (Easy) – Ascend the east side of the Needle, up the "safety steps" (ledges) designed by Clark Schurman to make this side easier for the "tyros" and "abecdarians." In his 1938 article, Schurman recommended avoiding the safety steps to make it more challenging. To that end, one can eliminate all of the ledges and any number of large holds to create dozens of possible variations, as easy or difficult as you please. Perhaps the most-difficult variation is to

climb the Needle with no hands; there are two no-hands variations, both with bad fall potential, in that you could crack your skull or some other appendage on a ledge or upon landing unless somebody's kid or dog breaks your fall.

"Safety Steps" (48) and "Needle Chimney" (15).

The Boulders.

TRAVERSE AROUND THE ROCK (Easy to Hard) — One can traverse all the way around Schurman Rock via several possible options. The easiest traverse is high up, foot-traversing the various ledges and hand traversing along the top edges of the walls; this version is easiest but high up so more risky. You can hand traverse the ledges instead, traversing around the rock at about mid-height; this is fairly straightforward except the section around the "SOUTH COLUMN" and "CHOCKSTONE CHIMNEY," where there are no ledges.

171

A traverse all the way around the base of the rock has some more-difficult sections, especially if you don't use the boulder at the base of the chimney as you pass through or any of the ledges. One lap around the rock involves about 80 feet of traversing; it's about ninety feet if you also traverse around the Needle. Of course, you can get creative and eliminate holds as you traverse, which makes traversing much more difficult. Give it a try using just twelve rocks as handholds, which is kind of hard but feasible. If you manage that, start eliminating to see how few rocks you can use to complete the full circuit. With judicious use of concrete holds and some creative no-hands moves, you might be able to complete the circuit using just six rocks for the hands.

THE BOULDERS – There are several large boulders scattered between the main rock and north tower, placed there to provide a place to practice "constant rhythmic running, surefootedness and familiarity with the slopes at which traction or adhesion is possible in different footwear," according to Clark Schurman. One may still use them to practice talus running and to test out new boots and rock shoes to get a feel for their friction coefficient, although a few of the boulders are kind of slippery now, so care should be taken not to go slipping off and cracking one's skull. They do provide a nice place to sit to change into rock shoes before a bouldering session, though.

NORTH TOWER – This is the small rock tower located just north of Schurman Rock. It's almost ten feet high at its highest, and is popular with the kids after they've been told to get down from the big rock, as if climbing on the smaller wall is so much safer given the many boulders to fall onto versus a flat landing on loose gravel around the main wall. (It isn't.) However, the North Tower is a good wall for kids to start bouldering; with a crash pad and spotter, bouldering is fairly safe on the tower since it isn't too high. As a bonus, the North Tower is usually open for climbing even if a group has reserved the main rock. If you drive out to Camp Long and find Schurman Rock closed for a climbing class, you may still be allowed to climb on the North Tower, which has several possible one-hand and no-hands problems and problems using only certain fingers on each hand that can keep even an experienced climber entertained, at least for a while. There are no-hands problems that use only a limited

172

number of rocks, and even one using only concrete holds. A no-hands traverse all the way around the base of the tower is challenging; it can be done in either direction.

The North Tower.

THE GLACIER – The Glacier is a companion feature to Schurman Rock, built in 1939-40 right after the climbing rock was completed. It is located about a hundred yards north of the rock via a wide ridgetop trail. It is something like an uneven, wide sidewalk running up a steep slope, built of out of the old granite ballast blocks that once were used to pave Seattle's streets, a sidewalk has been tilted up in places as if there was a violent earthquake that formed a series of slabs and steep walls. It was designed to mimic the features of a glacier icefall: crevasses, a serac, lateral moraines, and a bergschrund. The Glacier was designed to teach glacier travel and correct footwork on steep snow and ice slopes by use of "steps" formed on the steepest walls and embedded boot prints for students to follow, as well as ropework on snow, ice, and rock, and maintaining balance on irregular terrain.

The steeper slabs of the Glacier can be used for friction
climbing practice, balance, and footwork.

Rappelling lesson on the Glacier. Photo courtesy Mountain Madness.

Although the glacier is not used for glacier climbing practice much anymore, it is sometimes used for rappelling instruction, and can be used for conditioning for the big peaks. If you can't get out to Mount Si, just strap on a backpack full of rocks and hike up and down the Glacier or its lateral moraines for a few hours every day to get your legs in shape for a run up Mount Rainier. Even a half hour of hiking up and down the Glacier or its side trail is a good workout. One can also do a little bouldering on the steepest slabs, manteling up the "steps" using only your hands, palming up an arête, or friction climbing up the slabs without using the "steps."

Schurman Rock from the Parade Ground.

6.

CAMP LONG: FACILITIES, DIRECTIONS, AND ACCESS

SCHURMAN ROCK IS LOCATED AT CAMP LONG, at the 5200 block of 35th Avenue SW in West Seattle. To get there from downtown Seattle, take either I-5 or Highway 99 to the West Seattle Freeway, which leads west up the hill into West Seattle. Take a left at the first light (35th Ave SW) and follow 35th up the hill past the entrance to the golf course; the park entrance is on SW Dawson Street, the first left turn past the top of the hill. Look for the Camp Long signs. Park in the parking lot and hike east through the woods and over the meadow to the climbing rock. You can't miss it.

PARK RULES

Registering to climb on the rock is no longer required, but the park's website still asks that you check in before you climb, which is a good idea so you can find out if an organized group is scheduled that day. If you are planning a group outing you will want to reserve the rock for your event unless you are okay with sharing the rock with everybody and their dog. If the rock is reserved for a park or private group, it is closed to public use, so it is a good idea to call ahead to make sure it isn't booked before you drive there from any distance. Groups can also sign up to use the Challenge Course; check with the park for details. Park hours are generally 10 a.m. to 6 p.m. daily; however, Camp Long is closed on Mondays during the spring-fall season and Sundays and Mondays during winter months.

The park is gated and locked during off hours, so be sure to be out before closing time or you might get locked in; you may be able to squeeze out between the bars, but your car may be locked in overnight. Sneaking in when the park is closed is discouraged because it's illegal, and with more frequent police sweeps of the park due to homeless encampments, vandalism, and occasional gang activity, you're more likely to get cited for trespass than in years past. Although the gate may be open during the park's "closed" hours, the park is still closed. Campers and other groups can schedule use of the Lodge and other park facilities during off hours, but other visitors are not allowed. If you risk it, you could be locked in at any time.

Restrooms are located inside the Lodge, on the northwest side of the Parade Ground, and on the east side of the Parade Ground about 200 yards down the path north from the climbing rock. Please use them! They are generally open during park hours, but may be locked during the winter months on low-use days. If the outdoor restrooms are locked, head to the Lodge which is almost always open during park hours.

Dogs are required to be on leash at all times while in the park. Camp Long is a natural area with abundant wildlife, which is all too often disturbed by free-range dogs chasing after birds and squirrels. Also, no matter how friendly your dog may be, other people and dogs may not be as friendly, or may simply be afraid of dogs or not at all enamored of your approaching mutt. So, please keep your dog leashed, not only because it's the law, but as a courtesy to other park visitors. Also, please clean up after your dog! Bag that poop and dispose of it properly. A Seattle ordinance specifically prohibits dogs in playground areas, which includes climbing walls. Even if you have a well-behaved crag dog, please leave it at home or, if you must bring it, keep it on leash and tether it away from the rock so it doesn't bother any of the kids and other users of the rock or end up getting hurt when someone falls off and lands on it.

Although Seattle is a bike-friendly city, bike riding is not allowed at Camp Long. If you ride your bike to the park, you can lock it up at or near the Lodge. They might not mind if you walk your bike down the access road to the climbing rock, but please don't ride. Definitely no mountain biking on the trails since there are families with kids and people with dogs walking throughout the park, in addition to concerns about erosion on the sometimes steep, muddy paths. If you do bring your bike to the rock, please park it out of the way so people aren't tripping over or landing on it.

How many people can you get on Schurman Rock
at the same time? A lot!

Seattle has a drug and homeless problem that sometimes creeps into Camp Long. Be wary of homeless people who occasionally set up camp in or on the outskirts of the park, usually not near the rock, but they could be sleeping near the cabins or lurking around near the restrooms, especially early in the morning and later in the evening.

Used needles and other drug paraphernalia have been found in the park, so keep an eye out and report any illegal campers and potential hazards to park staff.

There has also been occasional gang activity in or near the park, mostly just tagging, occasionally on Schurman Rock itself. The park is usually very active during the day, with users doing all kinds of things all over the park—hiking the trails, walking dogs, using the Challenge Course, dropping off and picking up kids from day camps and preschool, doing park maintenance, and so on. Still, it's a good idea to pay attention to who's around and what they are doing, hike the trails with a buddy, and so on, the usual stuff you would do in any urban park to stay safe. Report any suspicious persons or vandalism to the park office or phone line listed below.

Finally, smoking and drinking are not allowed in the park, so leave those cigarettes and cans of Pabst Blue Ribbon at home. If you are one of those scofflaws who insists on smoking or drinking when you go climbing, please don't litter your butts or empties; dispose of them properly, and try not to set a bad example for the kids.

CAMP LONG CONTACT INFORMATION

Camp Long
5200 35th Ave SW
Seattle, WA 98126
(206) 684-7434
http://www.seattle.gov/parks/find/centers/camp-long

For a non-emergency, such as reporting a suspicious person or getting out if you've been locked in the park after hours, call 206-625-5011.

In case of emergency, dial 9-1-1.

CHALLENGE COURSE

Camp Long has a low- and high-ropes course, which is available for group reservations. Although some of the Challenge Course elements are tempting, please stay off of them unless you are accompanied by a trained facilitator. They are not playground equipment open for you or your kids to jump or bounce around on; they are designed for specific uses and cost quite a bit to install and repair. For information about the Challenge Course, or to reserve a group session, contact Camp Long.

LEAVE NO TRACE

Camp Long is usually a pretty clean place where polite visitors pick up and properly dispose of litter and dog poop. Please join us! It's easy to pick up litter and dispose of it properly in nearby trash and recycling receptacles, even if others haven't done so. Be a good steward and ambassador and clean up litter even if you didn't litter yourself; it makes a good impression and makes climbers seem like good, caring, environmentally conscious people. (Likewise, if you have a dog, don't be afraid to pick up someone else's dog poop, to avoid having other park visitors curse you and all dog owners for letting their dogs poop freely all over the park.)

If you fall off and leave a big divot in the gravel, please fill it back in for the next climber. If you use chalk, please brush off excess chalk after your session. Please clear gravel and leaves off the ledges and holds for the next climber and admonish your children not to throw gravel at each other or into the bushes.

Basically, treat Schurman Rock like it's your rock and leave it the way you would want to find it the next time you visit, so we can all continue to enjoy it.

Commemorative plaque atop Schurman Rock.

ACKNOWLEDGEMENTS

I USED TO CLIMB AT SCHURMAN ROCK back in the 1970s with my friend, Mark Gunlogson. We still climb here together occasionally, and together started Camp Long Mountain Fest in 2014 to celebrate the 75th Anniversary of Schurman Rock and Seattle's climbing history and community.

When I moved to the West Seattle area many years later, I returned to Camp Long and became reacquainted with Schurman Rock. After an afternoon bouldering session, I stumbled upon a gathering in the Lodge, where I was tricked into joining the Camp Long Advisory Council by Council members Mat McBride, Grace Bennett, David Kipnis, Jack Pedigo, Mary Quackenbush, Chas Redmond, and Dana Catts. But for them, I probably would not have learned so much about the history of the park and its outdoor programs, and become interested in maintaining the history and legacy of Schurman Rock. We have just started a new volunteer group, Friends of Camp Long, which, among other things, will help maintain Schurman Rock and the Glacier. Please join us!

This book would not have been possible without the assistance and support of Sheila Brown, Director of Camp Long, and Lowell Skoog, guardian of The Mountaineers' historical archives. They both provided historical information and many excellent photos for the book, and also reviewed and suggested improvements to the book during the editorial process.

Several people shared their remembrances of visiting Camp Long and climbing on Schurman Rock over the years, including Jim Whittaker, Lou Whittaker, Stuart Ferguson, Chuck Kelstrom, and Karen Daubert. Nancy Tegman shared her recollections of her kind gentleman neighbor, Clark Schurman. Laura Reason, Schurman's granddaughter, provided additional information and many of the photos that comprise the Camp Long collection.

Of course, I must acknowledge the contribution made by the many visitors to Camp Long, young and old, whom I have encountered at Schurman Rock over the past several years, who allowed me to eavesdrop on their climbing adventures, take their photos, and who unwittingly provided much of the material for the Schurman Rock Stories chapter.

And who could fail to acknowledge the contribution of Judge William G. Long, Archie Phelps, Ben Evans, and Clark Schurman? Not me. Only because of their vision and resolute dedication to creating a youth camp in Seattle is there even a climbing rock here to write about.

Finally, thanks the Camp Long and Outdoor Opportunities staff for keeping me informed of everything that happens at Schurman Rock, especially Yohann Hanley and Bob Warner, and to Mike Ayer, Per Nesselquist, Nic and Zoë Plemel, William Gates, Russ Erickson, and my other occasional climbing companions at Schurman Rock; to Mike Ayer, Trina Knable, and Beth Harman for their proofreading efforts and suggestions; and to Nick O'Connell for his tutelage and encouragement of my writing habit.

As always, thank you to my friends, family, and loved ones for their indulgence and to my parents for allowing me to run wild in the mountains in my youth.

ABOUT THE AUTHOR

Jeff Smoot is a writer and photographer primarily known for his hiking and climbing guidebooks including *Climbing Washington's Mountains*, *Rock Climbing Washington*, and *Best Climbs Cascade Volcanoes*. He has contributed to *Climbing*, *Rock & Ice*, *Backpacker*, and *Outside* magazines, and the *Western American Literature* journal. If it isn't raining, you might find him climbing on Schurman Rock.

Smoot, Jeff. *Pumping Concrete: A Guide to Seattle-Area Climbing Walls*. Seattle, WA: Stone Wall Media, 1996 (2d 2018).

Sundborg, George. "Troop 65: Boy Scout troop 'like no other' explored Unspoiled Puget Sound." *Magnolia News*, April 30, 1986.

Thornhill, Gary. "Climbing Walls and Other Animals"; "The World's First Artificial Climbing Wall, the Schurman Rock – Seattle – 1938-1940"; "Clark Schurman." GT World. June 13, 2017. http://www.gtworld.co.uk/schurmanrock.htm.

Whittaker, Lou and Gabbard, Andrea. *Lou Whittaker: Memoirs of a Climbing Guide*. Seattle, WA: Mountaineers Books, 1994.

Whittaker, Jim. A *Life on the Edge: Memoirs of Everest and Beyond*. Seattle, WA: Mountaineers Books, 1999.

——————. "The Trail to the Top of the World." *Boys' Life*, May 1978.

Unattributed. "Man-Made Peak Challenges Hardiest of Mountaineers." *The Seattle Star*, February 19, 1947.

——————. *Annual Report of the Department of the Interior*. US GPO, 1922-1930.

——————. "The Scout Camp in Wedgwood." Wedgwood in Seattle History Blog, February 27, 2012.

——————. "Boy Scouts of America." *Scouting*, Volume 8, Number 12, July 15, 1920, periodical, July 15, 1920; New York, New York. (texashistory.unt.edu/ark:/67531/metapth283174/: accessed June 13, 2017), University of North Texas Libraries, The Portal to Texas History, texashistory.unt.edu; crediting Boy Scouts of America National Scouting Museum.

The author in action on Schurman Rock.